HOW TO LEARN TO LIVE LIFE

"The journey of life is like an expedition, experience it closely"

MANISH MANNJYA

BlueRoseONE.com
Stories Matter
NewDelhi • London

BLUEROSE PUBLISHERS
India | U.K.

For permissions requests or inquiries regarding this publication, please contact:

BLUEROSE PUBLISHERS
www.BlueRoseONE.com
info@bluerosepublishers.com
+91 8882 898 898
+4407342408967

ISBN: 978-93-7018-494-7

Cover Design: Aman Sharma
Typesetting: Pooja Sharma

First Edition: June 2025

Dedication

I dedicate this book to my family members.

I have completed this book in the lap of serene environment of my Gurukul and have tried my best to express my thoughts in my own words. In this book, I have also shared the experiences of the past twenty years of my life. I hope this book will be beneficial to you.

-Author

Acknowledgment

I sincerely express my gratitude to all my family members who have taught me self-reliance over the past seven years. I also extend my thanks to those from whom I separated myself, taking a crucial step towards refining and elevating my thoughts.

I am grateful to all the friends and relatives I have met on this journey of life. Each of them has provided me with valuable lessons and inspiration, so that I could be able to get free myself from the narrow mentality. Over the years, I have worked in more than thirty companies, in various roles. I extend my heartfelt gratitude to all my colleagues, employees, and workers with whom I had the opportunity to spend time and gain invaluable experiences. A special thanks to the managers who recognized my abilities, appreciated my work, and encouraged me. Their support and guidance brought a significant transformation in my life, helping me find a successful path and consistently achieve my desired goals.

The greatest Influence in shaping my life's direction has come from the life stories of great personalities and the thoughts of successful individuals. Their inspiration and positive energy have given me new motivation every day. I deeply appreciate all the renowned writers, poets, and global speakers whose words have helped me navigate the challenges of life with greater ease.

I am also immensely grateful to Respected Kumar Vinit (Elder Brother) for his invaluable support in shaping this book into a well-structured form.

Finally, I bow with utmost reverence to the Almighty, whose divine grace has blessed me with the opportunity to write this book.

To live life, it is essential to be aware of the realities of life. Childhood has passed, adolescence has arrived, and even that is passing slowly with time. In fact, with the speed of time, we are not steering ourselves; we are simply being dragged along. Is this the right way? We are human, we have legs, and we possess a mind as vast as the ocean, with which we can walk and move forward. But why are we dragging ourselves along?

Wherever the crowd is going, we blindly follow, without knowing anything, we only know that the crowd is going that way. The truth is, our problems are not as big as we make them out to be. We repeatedly think about small problems and blow them out of proportion, but in reality, they are not that big.

Just like every parents says, my parents also used to say, "Study well, and you will become a good person." I remember that after completing my primary school up to the fifth grade in my village, I was enrolled in a government middle school about three kilometres away from the village. National festivals were celebrated at the school with cultural programs like plays, music, etc. For the first time, I participated, and it was on the 15th of August. The field was full of people, and my name was about to be called. Gathering courage, as soon as I went on stage, I forgot which song I was supposed to sing. My feet were trembling, and my heart was racing with fear.

Why is this happening? I had no idea. Just then, I remembered the song. The melody of the song was different, but I started singing it in a different tone. After a few minutes, I was off the stage and back home. That night, I couldn't sleep.

At that time, I must have been around eleven years old. I couldn't understand why I was feeling afraid. When I talk to a single person, I don't feel scared, but when hundreds of people are In front of me, where does the fear come from? These types of Thoughts were running through my mind. Perhaps this question also arises in many people's minds. Then I thought, "Will this continue to happen to me?" That was when I made my first decision in life: I had to overcome this fear. No matter what price I had to pay, I needed to prepare myself at that level. But how? I decided to be patient. This fear became the biggest obstacle in my life, and it is the biggest issue for everyone. One day, I discovered the secret to overcoming it. Today, whenever anyone talks to me about fear, I share this secret with them, and I'm sharing it in this book as well. I am confident by knowing this secret, you can overcome your inner fear and easily reach your goals, because most people are struggling with such issues. They are not living life, they are just passing through it. If you want to live such a life, you shouldn't forget that even animals do the same.

We are so entangled in our small, everyday tasks that we cannot get out of them. In our daily lives, whatever we do, it feels as if we are functioning in a state of sleep. We eat what's in front of us, we listen to whatever is playing, we watch whatever comes on screen, we say whatever words are spoken to us—whatever comes our way, we just keep doing it. And when the results come, we feel disappointed and wonder, "How did this happen?"

In this book, I've tried to explain both the situations that happen in human life and the right way to live. Today, we need the right mind-set and right thinking more than ever. We are going through difficult times, and sometimes it feels like life is slipping out of our control. This book will introduce you to life's principles that can give you the inner strength to handle challenges principles that only a few people truly know.

Life should not be lived with despair, but with enthusiasm and hope. We have limited time to live, and this book also highlights the importance of managing time wisely in our daily lives. We feel to be changed ourselves every day, but only some of us realize it. Everyone is chasing something in life, but the truth is, what they are looking for is already inside them. The important thing is recognizing it, and this book offers suggestions on how to do that.

Every person faces problems in life. This book gives useful advice on how to reduce those problems and how to make life happier while doing your daily duties. It also explains how to deal with people who feel jealous, angry, or egotistical to one another.

We often accept what others say or believe, whether it's right or wrong, without thinking. This book offers advice on how to choose what to accept and what to reject, which will help in your life.

Our thoughts shape who we are. How do thoughts form? We can create our thoughts the way we want, but how? These are also discussed in this book.

I have applied these secrets in my life, and I hope that by understanding them, you will be able to give your life a fresh start.

I begin this book with a poem I wrote, and I bow to nature, which has given us life and shelter.

Contents

Chapter 1

First Understand life then Start Living

If a person first understands the reality of life and then begins to live accordingly, life can become much easier and more fulfilling even when faced with a major problem, they can handle it with peace and confidence.

Are we truly happy with the work we are doing? If yes, then why do we feel so stressed? And if not, who is responsible for our unhappiness? We are working just to earn money and spending our valuable time on it. But think for a moment if one would give us the same amount of money, would we still choose to spend our time the same way?

Now, another question how much money do we actually need to live a good life? Pause for a moment and think about it. Why are we chasing money as if we are being carried away by the wind? This does not mean that money is unimportant, but I simply want to emphasize that money should be needed only as much as salt in food. When the right amount of salt is added, the food tastes good. Similarly, money has its rightful place in life, but only in the right proportion.

Balance in Life is Important

If we have too much money, life can lose its balance, just like adding too much salt can spoil the taste of food. This means that money should be in the right proportion for a happy life.

In today's fast-paced world, even doctors don't have solutions for all our problems. Common issues like stress, anxiety, fear, restlessness, weak memory, anger, and sadness often arise because we never truly learned how to live life properly.

I remember when I was in my first year of college, I read a book where a poet gave a beautiful example. Let me share it with you:

"If you try to pluck a rose with your eyes closed, the thorns will surely prick you. But if you first understand how a rose grows, recognize the distance between the thorns and the petals, then you can easily pick the flower without getting hurt."

Life works the same way. If we start living without understanding it, we will struggle with problems. But if we learn about life first, facing challenges becomes much easier.

Let's take another example. Imagine you want to collect honey. You must accept that bees will sting you. Similarly, if you aim to achieve something big in life, challenges will come. What truly matters is realising how to face them.

Today, in this competitive world everybody wants to get ahead of others, but very few people actually know where they are going. Many people today are in a race, trying to move ahead of others. But the reality is, very few know where they are actually going. They are just running without a clear destination. Imagine sending a letter without an address where will it go? Nowhere. It will remain undelivered. That's why having a clear goal in life is so important. When we know what we want, we can take the right steps to reach it.

From childhood, we accept whatever is taught to us right or wrong without questioning it. The way we speak, think, and behave is shaped by our surroundings. As we grow older, our experiences start shaping our thoughts. The things we see, the words we hear, and the environment around us influence us, even when we don't realize it. It is unfortunate that while a new-born infant cannot understand words, it only can feel its mother's emotions. But as it grows up, often witness its parents arguing sometimes over and over again. They hear harsh words and see negative behaviour. Without realizing it, the child absorbs all of this and starts to develop similar patterns.

That's why parents have a huge responsibility. The values and morals they teach their children shape their future. A child's foundation is built at home, and what they learn in their early years stays with them for life.

Understanding the Struggles of Growing Up

When a child reaches the age of 14 or 15, whether a boy or a girl, their body starts going through changes due to new hormones. It is natural for them to feel attracted to the opposite sex. However, this is also a critical age if their thoughts turn negative, they can easily be led in the wrong direction.

If a young person makes a serious mistake or commits a crime, their own family and society quickly start blaming them. But is it really their fault? I believe it is not. Even if they have done something wrong, the real question is who made them this way? The truth is, their family and society are responsible, not just the individual.

From childhood to adolescence, a person absorbs every thought and influence from his surroundings. When these thoughts lead to serious consequences, only then he realises the difference between right and wrong. By that time, he is already deeply entangled in negative thinking and feel trapped he begins to feel alone, lost, and sometimes even considers ending his life.

When they hit rock bottom, they start reflecting on their past, wondering, How did I become like this? How did I get so wrong? This self-awareness sparks a desire to truly understand life. Slowly they take steps toward a positive direction realising If I was shaped into something bad, I can also shape myself into something better.

But change is not easy. Negative thoughts keep pulling him back, making him feel like he is failing again and again. However, once he decides with strong determination to become a good and virtuous person, he starts making continuous progress. He seeks the company of wise and positive people those who are doing good in life.

In this journey, we often realize that we need ourselves more than anyone else and also this is true that we find easier to share our thoughts with friends than with our own family because our mind- set has become so distorted. Everyone wants to explain their point of view, but no one is ready to truly understand the other person.

The key is to first try to understand any situation before offering advice. Only then we guide others in a meaningful way.

Adapting to Change and Using Social Media Wisely

Everything is changing rapidly, and with time, the cost of living is also rising. If we do not adapt to these changes, we must be prepared to face challenges because avoiding them is not an option. Social media is both beneficial and harmful, especially for students. If not used wisely, it can have dangerous consequences that may not be visible immediately but will surely affect the future. It is important to use social media for good purposes; otherwise, it is better to stay away from it at least until you achieve your goals. Social media can easily lead you in the wrong direction. For example, companies use inappropriate images for advertising, and movies and songs are filled with vulgarity, which affects our minds every moment. It is necessary to stay away from such influences.

In society, we often witness fights between people. What do we do? We simply stand and watch. I used to do the same. But when I started understanding the value of life, I began questioning myself Where am I standing? What am I listening to? Who am I listening to? What am I watching? What will be the consequences? During these fights, people shout at one another, use harsh words, and create unnecessary chaos sometimes over minor issues like children arguing. Such small conflicts are seen everywhere, and we must learn to avoid getting involved in them.

Albert Einstein once said, "We cannot solve our problems with the same thinking we used when we created them." This reminds us that to overcome difficulties, we must change our mind-set and approach with wisdom.

There are two paths to learning and understanding life.

The First Path: We should seek a capable teacher or mentor who is experienced, whose thoughts are pure, elevated, and influential, and who truly understands life. This person should have done good deeds and be a source of inspiration for others. We can approach such a person someone who can understand our thoughts, recognize our confusions, and treat us with kindness and friendship. This will allow us to express ourselves freely and fearlessly, helping us understand life under their guidance. With their mentorship, we can strengthen our resolve and move forward towards our chosen goal.

The Second Path: This is a more difficult path. As we go through life, we can learn from our experiences and understand its realities. However, most people fail to grasp the deeper meaning of life. They stumble over small obstacles repeatedly, accepting life as it is without questioning its values. They neither attempt to understand life nor make an effort to seek knowledge, and eventually, they pass away without ever truly learning.

Some, however, face significant setbacks in life, which prompt them to ask deep questions: Why did this happen to me? How did it happen? If such an event occurred, how am I still alive? These thoughts lead them to deeper self-inquiry: Who am I? What is the purpose of my life? When these questions arise, a person becomes curious and starts seeking answers, embarking on the journey of learning and understanding life.

If we choose the first path early on, our journey becomes smoother, and life appears beautiful. Families will foster love and respect for one another. Every individual will naturally wish to honour and care for others. However, today's circumstances are such that, though people are born as humans, they often lose their humanity as they grow older. Instead of fostering love, many harbour feelings of resentment towards one another.

I have observed in many families that a person who earns well is respected, while another family member, who may not be as financially successful but is kind and virtuous, is treated differently. Reflecting on Other Aspects: The real question is why are we trying to change society when we haven't first tried to improve ourselves? If we work on bettering ourselves, our families will naturally improve, and society will transform on its own.

I frequently travel and interact with people. When I see individuals indulging in harmful habits like smoking or other addictions, I feel proud of myself for choosing a different path.

This realization strengthens my resolve to engage in meaningful and constructive actions. I even take a moment to thank myself, sometimes even bowing in gratitude, and then move forward with enthusiasm and determination in my work. If someone helps me in any way, I never forget to express my gratitude.

We live our lives surrounded by nature, but have we ever observed what the changing cycles of day and night, morning and evening, and the shifting seasons teach us? Could it be that human life follows a similar pattern? Happiness and sorrow, joy, wealth, and prosperity none of these remain permanent. They must change; this is the law of nature. When you truly understand this, you free yourself from greed and attachment. If we truly desire to understand life and live it in a beautiful and meaningful way, pay close attention to what I am about to share. Your age does not matter; what you have experienced up to this point is fine. I have understood the secret of life and started living accordingly, and now every new day feels like a festival to me. Life has become wonderful. At first, this felt like a mystery, but in reality, there is no mystery at all it's just that very few people pay attention to these truths, which is why they still seem hidden.

I am trying to share this secret with you, but to grasp it, you need to engage in some internal reflection. Prepare yourself for this process. Pause for a moment, calm your mind, and sit in solitude. If possible, drink a glass of cool water. During this practice, avoid any external noise, and close your eyes. Now you are ready let's begin. Go back in time for a moment and try to recall three major events from your past events that had a significant positive or negative impact on your life.

First, let's consider some negative experiences. These could be anything for example, a long-standing relationship that suddenly ended, leaving both people separated. Another example could be a conflict over property or wealth that led to a dispute within the family or with neighbours, even resulting in someone's death. Or imagine being wrongly imprisoned for some time, even if you were innocent.

Now, let's recall some positive experiences moments that brought you great happiness. Maybe your work was widely appreciated, and you received an award, bringing you immense joy. Or perhaps you helped feed the hungry and assisted the needy. Maybe you once saved someone from drowning, or you contributed significantly to the well-being of your community. Or perhaps you served as a capable teacher, making a meaningful impact on a larger scale.

Next, reflect on your present day. Think about everything you did today the people you met, the conversations you had, and any events that happened, whether good or bad. If you felt exhausted by the day's events, you likely fell into a deep sleep as soon as you lay down.

Now, let's move to the final event I want you to reflect upon. Imagine your last night, when you fell into deep sleep and started dreaming whatever good or bad things occurred in that dream, do you remember them? If so, those dreams were simply reflections of the thoughts and emotions you carried throughout the day.

I have observed that some people talk in their sleep as if they are having a conversation with someone. Others wake up suddenly, shouting in fear due to a nightmare. Their bodies tremble with fright. Some even start walking in their sleep, just like scenes from movies but this is real. All these experiences your past memories, today's events, and your dreams are now behind you. Take a moment to reflect on them.

Now, I want you to do something: write them down on a piece of paper. Keep this paper private do not show it to anyone. It will contain the significant good and bad moments of your life. Safeguard it and keep it confidential. This will serve as a record of your past actions and experiences, just as illustrated in Table 0.01.

S/NO	GODDS DEEDS & THEIR CONSEQUENCES	EVIL DEEDS & THEIR CONSEQUENCES
1		
2		
3		
4		
5		

Table 0.01

S/NO	WORK DONE IN PRESENT TIME	LAST NIGHT DREAM
1		
2		
3		
4		
5		

Table 0.02

On another sheet of paper, write down the activities you carried out today and yesterday, as well as the dreams you had last night, as I mentioned earlier. Just like Table 0.02, this will help you see a summary of the results of your actions over the past few years. Now, take a moment to carefully review this list. Think about how you interacted with your friends, relatives, society, family members, and colleagues. How was your behaviour towards them? You spend time with your family, but most of your day is spent at the office, school, or with friends. By now, you might have started to understand the purpose of these exercises Tables

0.01 and 0.02 contain your past and present actions. Both the right and wrong actions are in front of you.

Now, carefully consider the following questions. If most of your answers lead in a positive direction, then 95% of your actions listed in the table are correct. However, if only a few answers align, it indicates that some of your actions were incorrect.

Questions About Friendship:

1. Is your friend's character and behaviour better than yours?
2. Does your friend appreciate your good actions?
3. Can you use your friend as an example when talking to others and say, "I want to develop a character like him"?
4. Do you feel happy when talking to your friend?
5. Has your friend ever refused to help you in a difficult situation?
6. Do you prefer making friends only with people of your age?
7. Are your friend's thoughts pure and inspiring?

I understand that some of these answers may be either "yes" or "no."

Questions About Family:

1. If you want to achieve something good in life, do your parents support you?
2. Do small arguments frequently occur in your family?
3. Is your family financially stable?
4. Do you feel peaceful with your family?
5. Are your family members engaged in good deeds?
6. Does anyone in your family have bad habits, such as substance abuse?
7. Do your family members show love and respect toward each other?
8. Does anyone in your family harbour jealousy toward another member?
9. Would you like to become like someone in your family in the future? If not, why?
10. Is the environment of the society you live in positive and healthy?

In Table 0.02, you have listed all the activities you did throughout the day, the thoughts that occupied your mind, and the dreams you had at night, which were influenced by your daily thoughts. After completing this exercise, you will have a clearer understanding of the path you are walking in life.

If, after answering these questions, you realize that changes are needed, take a firm resolution and choose the right path. In the beginning, shifting from one path to another where your answers are positive will bring challenges and difficulties. However, once you make the change, you will ultimately gain wealth, happiness, prosperity, and success. If you do not change your path, you will continue to struggle with problems throughout your life. The decision is in your hands either improve your life and give it a meaningful direction or continue as before. There is no alternative.

Do not try to suppress this energy, as that would go against nature. Instead, align yourself with nature. Once you set your life in the right direction, observe how vast and powerful this energy truly is. Life is meant to be lived, not suffered. As intelligent beings, we must develop the wisdom to understand things correctly only then we can avoid confusion and live a fulfilling life.

<u>**Summary**</u>

1. The most valuable things in life air, sunlight, water, fire, and fertile soil are freely given to us by nature. Always be grateful to the Creator for these gifts.
2. Positive thoughts are many times more powerful than negative ones. By thinking positively, we can change even the worst situations in our lives.
3. Reflect on past mistakes that are causing problems in your present life. Write them down and work on resolving them first.
4. To live a good life, it is essential to surround ourselves with the right people.
5. We are the masters of our own lives. Blaming others for our problems is stupidity.
6. When a person acknowledges their mistakes, they find the right direction in life.

On this journey of life, having an ideal guide is important. That guide is within us, but to recognize it, we need the wisdom and direction of an authentic teacher or mentor.

Chapter 2

What to Accept and What Not to Accept from Others

"A strong character is built only after facing thousands of obstacles."

- Swami Vivekananda

When a child is born in a family, after some time (months), everyone except the mother is introduced to the child one by one. he is told, "This is your father," "These are your grandparents." However, there is no need to introduce the mother because the child is formed from her very body. His emotions are naturally connected to his mother from birth. When he feels discomfort, the mother instinctively understands why he is crying and fulfils his needs. It is the mother who tells the child, "This is your father," and the child accepts it.

As the child grows, he quickly learns whatever is taught to him in his early years because a child's brain functions exceptionally fast during that phase. By the time he reaches the age of ten or twelve, whatever he has been told repeatedly gets embedded in his subconscious mind. He accepts the language, customs, and traditions of his family and society as his own, believing, "This is who I am." If he is born into a Hindu family, he identifies as Hindu. If born into a Muslim family, he considers himself as Muslim. In the same way, he accepts the environment in which he is raised without ever questioning why things are the way they are.

He never pauses to ask: Why is the earth below and the sky above? Why am I living in the midst of nature? What are all these religions and sects?

Regardless of which religion one follows, it is essential to first understand the fundamental duty of being human. Once a person comprehends this, they realize that spending time trying to understand different religions may not be as significant as fulfilling their duty as a human being. The wise quickly grasp that the soul is eternal it has always existed and never truly perishes; only the body undergoes change.

A student possesses limitless potential, but most of the time, they misuse their abilities. This happens because they face many confusions and dilemmas they struggle to understand what is right and what is wrong. Nowadays, students often find themselves stuck in such mental conflicts, unable to break free.

For nearly fourteen to fifteen years, they have been accepting the thoughts and opinions of others as truth. Their mind-set is shaped by these influences, and they believe them to be the ultimate reality. But let me tell you if everything you have accepted so far has come from others, then why do you hesitate or feel afraid when moving forward? The reason is simple: you lack the right information because you are still unaware of life's realities.

Now, the important question is who are the people who have advised you throughout your life? Have you ever thought about this? Most of the time, they are family members or relatives. But the mistake many people make is accepting their advice without questioning it.

You have intelligence, so why not use it? Before accepting advice, take a moment to observe the life of the person giving it. If you had done this earlier, you could have avoided many wrong ideas. Often, people accept advice simply because the advisor knows slightly more than them. However, it is crucial to evaluate whether the advice is truly correct and to what extent it applies to your situation.

You must have noticed that within your family and relatives, you receive many different pieces of advice. Sometimes, you follow them without questioning, and while some may lead to positive outcomes, others might misguide you. For example, imagine you are traveling to a new place and ask someone for directions. If that person deliberately gives you wrong directions, you might follow them without realizing they are wrong. As a result, you waste both time and energy. This is why paying attention to such small details is important.

Another common challenge students face is choosing their career path. Many students, even at the age of thirty, still struggle to decide what career suits them best. As a result, they end up taking any available job without proper direction. The root cause of this confusion is that they rely on advisors who have not achieved anything significant in their own lives. Ironically, it is often inexperienced people who are the quickest to give advice. We will discuss these important facts in detail in the next chapter.

Nowadays, in almost every household, you will find at least one person who is addicted to some kind of substance. You must have heard them talk–they fail to understand that consuming intoxicating substances harms their body. Instead, they seek taste and pleasure in these harmful things.

If they truly realized the damage these substances cause, they would never consume them. However, many people continue their addiction even after knowing the harmful effects. Sadly, regret only comes later when they are already suffering from a serious disease. But the question is, why this stubbornness?

First Principle : Be Mindful of Whose Advice You Follow

If someone whether a friend, relative, or anyone else gives you advice but is addicted to harmful substances, you should not take their words seriously. Such a person lives within a limited and negative mind-set and tries to influence others to live the same way.

If you, too, have any addiction, just look at the results it's already affecting your life. But if you break free from that limited mind- set, you can achieve much greater things.

Life is Beautiful Don't Waste It

Life is precious, so don't let it slip away. Make an honest effort to live it fully, and you will see how beautiful it is. The real problem is that we avoid thinking for ourselves.

We often have simple solutions to our problems but still rely on others to handle them. And when those people make mistakes, we end up spending more time and energy fixing them. This happens because we depend too much on others instead of taking responsibility ourselves. From childhood, we are conditioned to accept what others say without question. But no bad habit forms overnight it always has a deeper story behind it.

In reality, everyone has a good side. No one wants to become a bad person. But then, how does someone not only become bad but even lead a group of wrongdoers?

I remember when I left my village after completing my matriculation and moved to the city for my polytechnic studies. Everything was new to me living in a hostel, attending college on time it all felt exciting. However, I was uncomfortable with the behaviour of some senior students. As soon as college was over for the day, many would step outside and smoke, along with other bad habits. Some even smoked inside the hostel, blowing smoke right in my face. It made me angry, but I reminded myself that I had come all this way to study, so I controlled myself .

I complained to the principal several times, but nothing changed because the majority of students behaved the same way. Eventually, I decided to leave the hostel and move to a PG accommodation near the college, hoping it would be better. But I was wrong. The environment there was even worse. The rent was cheaper, so many students stayed there just to pass time rather than focus on studies.

As my first year was coming to an end, I started looking into the career paths of students who had graduated. Some had jobs, but many struggled due to low marks or a lack of skills. Some took four to five years to complete a three-year course, while others got jobs with extremely low salaries. Around 90% of the students were facing these issues.

By then, I had had enough. I realized that this kind of education was leading me nowhere. Without wasting any more time, I made the bold decision to quit the college. It felt meaningless to continue down a path that wasn't taking me in the right direction.

If you ever feel that you're heading in the wrong direction, stop and change course. There's no point in banging your head against a wall it only hurts you, not the wall.

Remember, *life is full of opportunities, just like the ocean is full of waves.* But the problem is, we rarely try to search for them. Since childhood, we have been conditioned to depend on others' opinions and advice. It's time to break free from that mind-set and become self-reliant.

Be Careful Who You Trust

You may have noticed that when some people meet you for the first time, they speak very sweetly and politely. Most people get carried away by this.

For example, suppose you go to a new city for a job opportunity. Someone in an office warmly welcomes you, praises the company, and convinces you that it's a great opportunity. You believe them, feel excited, and even give them money or personal documents if they ask.

But what happens next? When you return later, you find that there's no office, no employees, and no way to contact the person you met. Then you say, "I was cheated!"

But if you think carefully, you'll realize that no one truly deceived you you deceived yourself. Actually The world is full of such scammers, yet you trusted someone without verifying anything. The real mistake was blindly believing their words.

The result? You end up suffering a loss. Such fraudsters exist everywhere some operate online, others offline. The key is to stay aware and cautious so that you don't fall into their traps.

Second Principle: Be Cautious of Sweet Words

When someone speaks to you politely and with kindness, there is often a hidden motive behind it. That motive can be anything. You must also remember that the things that attract you the most often have the potential to cause the greatest harm.

So, if someone is being overly kind or respectful toward you, don't rush to trust them. Instead, try to gather as much information as possible about them it will be in your best interest.

I remember an experience from my time in Gujarat. On a special occasion, I gave a gift to a friend. To my surprise, he refused to accept it. At first, I felt a little hurt, but then he explained his reason. He said, "The greatest gift you can give someone is your time nothing else matters more to me." His words surprised me.

However, I still believe that if someone offers you something out of love, you should accept it. A gift is not just an object; it carries the emotions and affection of the person giving it.

Third Principle: Accept Yourself as You Are

The first step to self-confidence is accepting yourself exactly as you are. Everything you have, from birth until now, is a part of you, and you should embrace it rather than trying to change it based on societal expectations.

I have seen many boys and girls who feel embarrassed about their height. They try different methods to appear taller, influenced by countless advertisements promising miraculous results. But height is not a problem it is simply how their body is designed.

Similarly, some girls worry about their short hair, trying various oils and treatments to make it longer and thicker. Others use fairness creams, hoping to change their skin colour. In reality, these are temporary solutions, often causing more harm than good.

Focusing too much on these external things distracts you from your real goals. You waste your time, money, and energy on something unnecessary instead of working on what truly matters. Even worse, when people around you make comments about your appearance, you start feeling ashamed and anxious.

But ask yourself why are you not happy with what you already have? Why do you let small things make you feel insecure? The real reason is that you have never looked at yourself through your own eyes. Instead, you have always seen yourself through the eyes of others.

Once you stop seeking validation from others and start embracing yourself as you are, you will realize that your uniqueness is your greatest strength.

Embrace Life with Gratitude

Friends, nature has created each of us in a unique way and sent us to this Earth for a limited time. Instead of complaining, we should accept this gift with joy and express gratitude every day for being alive and healthy. Each morning when we wake up, we should thank the divine power that allows us to see another day. With nearly eight billion people on this planet, many go to bed at night but never wake up again.

Some believe that life is measured by age, but in reality, it is measured by our breaths. Every moment, every hour, every day our breaths are being counted. Over months, years, and decades, the total is predetermined, and one day, those breaths will stop.

That's why we should focus on appreciating what we have instead of worrying about what we lack. With effort and determination, we can achieve many things. The key is to live each day with gratitude and celebrate life as a festival, making the most of every moment.

Summary

1. Some things in life don't require proof love and trust in a person are enough.
2. We are perfectly created by nature; there is no need to change our physical appearance.
3. Before accepting anyone's advice, gather the right information about them; if their guidance isn't beneficial, feel free to reject it.
4. If we don't have the power to change a negative environment, we should change our surroundings instead.
5. No living being on this Earth is given a fixed lifespan only breaths. Life isn't counted in years but in the number of breaths we take.

Chapter 3

How to Prevent Mental Illnesses

"Health is the greatest wealth, contentment is the greatest treasure, and self-confidence is the greatest friend." – Lao Tzu

The word "mental" refers to the mind, meaning that whatever we imagine in our thoughts directly impacts our body and mind, both internally and externally. Mental illnesses primarily arise due to stress and include conditions such as depression, anxiety, panic attacks, excessive fear, irritability, fatigue, memory loss, and many more.

In today's fast-paced world, people suffer more from mental health issues than physical illnesses. Many seek help from psychiatrists and psychologists to find relief. If we observe, urban populations are more affected by mental health disorders compared to rural areas. Nowadays, almost every family has at least one member suffering from some form of mental distress.

Let's explore how these mental health problems begin. When a person reaches the age of 15 or 16, he starts feeling the weight of responsibilities improving their family's financial situation, choosing a career, maintaining friendships, planning for marriage, and facing numerous life challenges. For a middle-class child, overcoming these struggles can be overwhelming. However, I do not want to label it solely as a "middle-class issue" because such challenges are universal.

The Importance of Mental Diet

Life without struggles is incomplete. Every person faces challenges some stumble, while others overcome them and truly enjoy life. But how do mental illnesses develop? How does a person go wrong?

To maintain energy, humans consume two types of nourishment: one for the body and another for the mind. However, most people are not aware of how they feed their minds, which is their biggest mistake. How does this happen? Let's understand:

The first thing people do is feed their minds without awareness. You might wonder how can the mind be fed? Just like our body needs nutritious food, our mind also requires healthy and positive content. However, we often neglect this.

For example, as soon as we wake up, we start reading newspapers filled with all kinds of negative news violence, crime, tragedies, or failed love stories where someone ends their life. Some people even enjoy reading scandalous or explicit content. With the internet, access to negativity has become effortless. People of all ages, from children to the elderly, consume such content without realizing its long-term effects.

Now, pause and think if this is what we feed our minds daily, what will be the result? Our mind is like soil; whatever seeds we plant will determine what grows. Just like planting a mango seed will never give you grapes, the thoughts and content we consume shape our mental state. As the Bible says, "You reap what you sow."

But when you receive the results of your actions, why do you feel sad and disappointed? Why do you suffer from various mental health issues? This is related to what I call the first diet of life. If you truly want to stay away from these mental struggles, you must pay special attention to your first diet.

This world is like a marketplace of thoughts. Only human beings have the ability to differentiate between good and bad thoughts. Every thought, every image we see, everything we hear or read these are like seeds being planted in the soil of our minds. You have the power to nurture and shape them as you wish.

Now, how can you practically use this first diet in your daily life? How can you understand it more easily? Let's consider the following key points:

1. Avoid unnecessary news and negative information as much as possible in the morning.
2. Develop a habit of reading inspiring books or biographies of great personalities.
3. Stay away from obscenity and inappropriate content as much as possible.
4. Avoid unnecessary crowds and do not get entangled in minor conflicts, as they can hold you back in life.
5. Never stay in places where there is no meaningful discussion or logical exchange of thoughts.

Let's come to another point as our mind requires a proper diet to stay mentally strong, our body also needs nutritious food to remain strong and energetic.

What Should We Eat? Understanding the Right Diet for the Body, many questions arise. It is generally agreed that we should consume nutritious food that provides energy and keeps the body healthy. Scientists also support this idea.

However, when it comes to eating meat, the question arises is it right or wrong?

Humans are the only species on Earth with the ability to understand what is right and wrong. We have the power to experience emotions and understand the feelings of others. In today's modern world, many people keep pets dogs, cows, goats, rabbits, parrots, peacocks, and many more. Not only do they take care of these animals, but they also develop a deep emotional bond with them, even talking to them.

Now, Many thoughts may be running through your mind right now. Calm yourself and ruminate do you think the creatures living on this Earth experience emotions just like us? Of course, they Just like humans, they feel happiness, sadness, and even anger.

But what happens when a human kills an animal? Do you think that animal feels joy? Does it laugh? Absolutely not. Just like us, it experiences emotions such as fear, hatred, pain, anger, and sorrow. Its entire body vibrates with that negative energy. And what do humans do? They bring that negativity-filled meat home, cook it, and consume it as food.

When that food enters the body, it carries the same negative vibrations, leading to emotions like anger, restlessness, anxiety, and hatred. Unfortunately, most people fail to recognize this impact. They assume that eating meat gives them energy and keeps them healthy. But in reality, it invites numerous illnesses especially mental disorders that even doctors struggle to cure.

Many diseases stem from stress, depression, anger, fear, and anxiety, which prevent us from progressing in life. People often fail to understand this connection until they find themselves surrounded by these problems. Only then do they realize the truth.

The Simple Truth: A Blown-Out Candle Cannot Light Another Candle

If we want to protect ourselves from these illnesses, we must nourish our bodies with pure, vegetarian food. By now, you have learned about the two types of diets that significantly impact our mental well-being.

Some may argue, "But I already follow a vegetarian diet! Why do I still experience these mental struggles?" The answer is simple: you are only focusing on the second type of diet the physical one. However, to truly heal, you must also take care of the first diet the diet of the mind.

When you balance both types of diets in your life, you will witness miraculous changes within days. Your life will start improving, and you will feel a noticeable reduction in mental stress and negativity.

The secret of fear

This issue is particularly common among young people and often becomes the biggest obstacle in their journey through life. However, this topic is rarely discussed in coaching institutes, colleges, or other educational institutions. You might have only heard a speaker mention it in a seminar. But why don't teachers talk about it? Why isn't it included in the student curriculum?

Think about a young child you'll notice that he has no fear at all. But as he grows older, fear begins to take root in his mind. Eventually, he becomes burdened with countless fears that he struggles to overcome for the rest of his life.

For example, a student may go for an exam, knowing all the answers, yet forget everything due to fear. The thought of "What if I fail or get low marks?" paralyzes his mind.

Similarly, someone preparing for a job interview might be well- qualified, but as soon as they sit in front of the interviewer, fear takes over. He begins to doubt himself, "What if I fail the interview and don't get the job?"

Some people are afraid of speaking in public, while others are afraid of snakes or scorpions or any animal, thinking "If they bite me, I'll die." A married man might afraid of losing his beautiful wife, thinking "What if she leaves me?" Some fear taking their wife shopping, worried about "How much will she buy?" Then there's fear of illness, financial loss, and countless other anxieties that appear in life.

However, have you ever tried to understand where fear comes from? The truth is, we were not born with these fears. They developed over time due to the influence of others around us. Yet, very few people actually stop to question the nature of fear.

Now, let's try to remove this mysterious veil of fear once and for all.

Understanding and Overcoming Fear

Fear is a natural human emotion but to what extent is it justified? If you are living with honesty, discipline, and the right values, you have nothing to fear. However, when you act unethically or have negative thoughts, fear naturally takes control of you. Once you understand these causes, you can break free from fear.

I, too, struggled with fear during my college years, and it was my biggest weakness. By then, I was never taught how to deal with fear. Speaking in front of a crowd felt impossible for me.

I still remember my first day in class when the teacher asked me to introduce myself I was so nervous that I couldn't even speak properly.

But one day, I understood that fear is just an illusion. Today, I can speak in front of thousands of people without hesitation. I have cleared multiple job interviews with confidence.

How did this transformation happen? Let's uncover the secret to overcoming fear.

If you take a moment to look at life from a different perspective, you will realize that this world is a grand stage, and each of us is merely playing a role for a limited time. The moment we are born, we become a part of this great play, and we will continue to perform until the end of our lives.

Now, pause and think what kind of character do you want to play in this grand drama? Ultimately, the choice is yours. Life is a one- time opportunity, and once it's gone, you won't get another chance.

When I first understood this concept, I made a firm decision to fight my fears. I broke free from the limitations that had confined me for so long. One of my biggest fears was speaking in front of a crowd. But instead of running away, I made a resolution: I will overcome this fear forever.

At that time, I was in 12th grade, and I actively looked for opportunities to speak or sing at events whether in my village, nearby towns, college functions, or national celebrations.

I stopped worrying about what people would think of me. Instead, I reassured myself that mistakes are natural in the beginning. To ease my nerves, whenever I stepped onto a stage, I would start by apologizing in advance: "If I make any mistakes, please forgive me." This simple mind-set helped me step out of my comfort zone and break free from fear.

I had a strong determination that fear should have no place between me and my goal. Yes, I had to read and memorize many things for this, but even today, I carry the same passion. In this drama-like world, I am just a temporary character so why not give my best performance? For me, finding the right path was essential and now, I have found it. When you start comparing yourself to others, you limit your own potential and abilities. That's why you should never compare yourself with others. The only comparison you should make is with yourself how can you improve from yesterday? How can you do better than before?

Over time, my fear has slowly transformed into confidence. Today, if I see someone feeling sad, scared, or anxious, I ask them, "Hey, why is there no comedy in your play these days?" Do you know that fear in life comes in two forms imaginary fear and real fear? Let's understand this with some examples.

Imaginary fear arises from our thoughts. As I mentioned earlier, we often fear small things like snakes, scorpions, or insects. These creatures are tiny compared to us, and a single strike can eliminate them. But we have heard since childhood that they are poisonous and can be deadly. But it is also true that fear increases the chances of harm even more.

Scientists have extensively studied the human brain. The way we think directly affects the production of different hormones in our brain, which then influences our body's reactions. Our brain is like a machine whatever we focus on, it starts working in that direction instantly, often without us realizing it.

When you confine yourself within a limited mind-sets and suddenly face something beyond those boundaries, fear takes over. That's why you should never restrict yourself your mind is as vast as the open sky. So why try to limit it?

The moment you compare yourself to others thinking "That person is rich, but I am poor," or "They are smart, and I am not like him," you start losing confidence. But the truth is, no one is born rich or poor, intelligent or slow. We all start the same way. Everyone is given two eyes, two hands, and two legs so what is there to compare?

You should always remember that only you can play your role in life no one else can do it for you. So, where is the need to be afraid? Seventy percent of the fears we experience are imaginary, and you don't need to be afraid of them at all. Now, you might ask, "What is real fear?" Let's understand this with an example.

Imagine you are on a flight to another country. The journey is supposed to last two hours. After just 30 minutes, the plane's engine catches fire, and the pilot loses control. In this situation, fear is natural because the risk of death is real.

Apart from such real dangers, fear has no place in life. I repeat if you have the right mind-set, follow positive principles, and live with discipline, fear will not control you.

The Importance of Laughter and Dance in Life

Who likes a sad or gloomy face? No one. People do so much just to laugh and stay happy. Have you ever noticed how joyful parents feel when they see their children laughing? It's as if they have found everything they ever wanted.

You may have observed that people who don't laugh much often struggle with mental health issues. Their faces show signs of stress, and they always seem serious. To feel happy and reduce stress, they sometimes attend comedy shows or laughter clubs. But did you know that many mental health issues can be relieved simply by laughing or dancing?

Everyone should take some time each day to laugh and dance. It fills the body with fresh energy and helps maintain good health. However, people often chase negative things for entertainment and forget what truly benefits them. Instead, why not listen to spiritual music like the *Hare Krishna Hare Krishna, Krishna Krishna Hare Hare, Hare Ram Hare Ram Ram Ram Hare Hare* chant and dance to it? It will bring you positive energy and peace of mind.

I have a different approach I sometimes remember a funny or positive moment from my life and start laughing loudly, no matter where I am. Whether I'm with my family or in a group of strangers, some people are surprised by my reaction. But soon, without even knowing why, they start laughing with me!

I never miss a chance to laugh because it refreshes the mind. Have you ever seen a donkey laugh or smile? No! Laughter is a special gift that only humans have been given. So, laugh freely and spread joy around you. This will not only help you, but also uplift those around you!

<u>Summary</u>

1. Mental illnesses often stem from stress. You can reduce stress by laughing, dancing, or shifting your thoughts towards positivity.

2. Instead of comparing yourself to others, compare your present with your past achievements to see how you can improve.
3. Most people spend their lives trapped by fear, like a frog in a well. Wise individuals, however, constantly strive to reach new heights in life.
4. Since we are already part of this play called life, aim to play a role that sets an inspiring example for others.
5. Paying attention to small mistakes can eventually lead to significant positive changes in your habits.

Chapter 4:
How to Set Goals in Life

"Whenever we start something new in life, it's natural to feel confused or afraid. But instead of getting discouraged, we should face these feelings with courage".

I remember when I was in school, my friends and I would often talk casually about our plans for the next day. Most of the time, it was just about completing homework or discussing games nothing special. But if there was a plan to go somewhere during school or college holidays, the excitement was different. After all, who doesn't enjoy traveling to new places? However, for me, meeting new people and having conversations with them was just as exciting as exploring new destinations. Even when guests visited our home, I would listen to them carefully, observing their way of speaking and their communication style. I was always curious to learn about them. But if I didn't find their conversation interesting, I would quietly walk away.

During school days, I noticed that students who completed their college education would either prepare for government job exams or, if their families were not financially stable, look for private jobs. Some would move to different cities for higher studies. I was always eager to meet new people and understand their perspectives. Often, I would ask them, "Have you completed your studies?" They would reply, "Not yet, I still need a year or two." Then I would ask, "What will you do after that?" Most of them would hesitate for a moment and say, "I'll think about it later" or "Let's see what happens." Their uncertainty surprised me, but I realized that this was a common response among students.

After completing their education, most young people are primarily focused on earning more money. Very few consider starting a business because they believe it is beyond their capability. The common perception is that business requires a lot of money, which many don't have.

Today, most students find themselves in a dilemma. Even after completing their studies, they struggle to decide what they truly want to do in life or which direction to take. Their minds are filled with conflicting thoughts, and many spend years preparing for job exams. Some people continue their education until they cross the age of thirty, yet still struggle to find a stable and well-paying job. Even those who do secure jobs often lose interest in their work after a few years. The very profession they worked tirelessly to enter no longer brings them satisfaction.

This lack of clarity and direction is one of the biggest challenges young people face today. Understanding one's true goals in life is essential to avoiding this uncertainty and finding lasting fulfilment.

Understanding Career Choices and Goal Setting

In the northern parts of India, many students share a common mindset they are determined to secure a government job by any means necessary, even if it means taking up any position just to be employed. But is this the right approach? How valid is the belief that getting a government job is the ultimate goal of life? I am not saying that government jobs are bad or that one should not prepare for them. However, we must first recognize that with the rapid increase in population, competition for every opportunity has become fierce. The question is are you preparing with this reality in mind? Most people are not.

A few months ago, I met a stranger who was a software engineer working at a prestigious company. He had a high-paying job and had spent five years in the industry. Yet, he was not satisfied with his work and was now trying to become a Sanskrit teacher. Just two days later, I met a teacher who was saying the exact opposite he found office jobs more appealing and was preparing for a different career, leaving his teaching profession behind.

Why do people spend years preparing for a career, only to later change their minds? The answer lies in the fact that people seek variety in their work. But there is another crucial question when you chose your career, was it truly your own decision, or were you influenced by someone else? Many people follow a particular career path just because they see others doing it. If your decision was truly personal, you wouldn't want to change it so easily.

This is how many go towards wrong directions Instead of focusing on personal interest and passion, they choose a career based on financial gains and job availability. However, they forget the most important factor interest. When you step into a field without genuine interest, you eventually lose motivation and become dissatisfied with your work.

So, why do we blindly follow others? Just because someone else is successful in a field doesn't mean it is right for you. That person may have a deep passion for the work, which is why they are happy and thriving. You, on the other hand, might be forcing yourself into something that doesn't truly excite you.

Let's understand this with an example. A person who wants to become a skilled doctor must study human anatomy in depth. To achieve this, they invest years of time, effort, and money. But what drives them? Their deep-seated interest and a strong sense

of purpose. Their confidence in their chosen field keeps them motivated. Such a doctor sees their profession as a service rather than just a job. Every time they treat a patient, they pray for strength to heal them. This sense of fulfilment makes their work meaningful, and they feel grateful that their life serves a greater purpose.

The point is simple don't let others' choices dictate your life. Choose a career that truly interests you, one that brings you inner satisfaction and joy. When you work with passion and purpose, success and happiness will follow naturally.

The Power of Clear Decision-Making

When you decide on a goal, don't just think about it once think about it a hundred times before committing. The problem is that most people have too many different thoughts running through their minds. They think, "If this doesn't work out, I'll try something else." This mindset prevents them from fully dedicating themselves to a single goal, and as a result, they never reach their true destination.

True commitment means having no alternative to your goal. If you want to achieve something, the first step is to be absolutely clear about what you want and why you want it. Ask yourself:

- What am I trying to achieve?
- Why is it important?
- How will it benefit me and others?

Once you define your goal, set a time frame for achieving it. This helps create urgency and focus. The timeline will depend on how big the goal is, but without a deadline, progress becomes uncertain.

For example, suppose you need money. Simply wishing for it won't help you need to determine exactly how much you need and how you will earn it. Without clarity, you can't take effective action. This is why proper planning is crucial before starting any task.

Example 1: Constructing a Building

Before constructing a large building, professionals like engineers and architects are consulted. They inspect the land, create blueprints, and carefully plan every detail. A timeline is set for completion to ensure smooth execution and avoid future problems. Without this structured approach, the building would never be completed efficiently.

Example 2: Reaching a Destination

Imagine you want to travel to a specific place, but you don't know the exact address. How will you ever reach your destination? You might wander aimlessly or take the wrong path, making it difficult to return. The same applies to life without a clear goal, you can't achieve anything. Even small tasks become difficult if there is no strong determination behind them.

Many people procrastinate, thinking, "If it doesn't happen today, I'll do it tomorrow." Or they abandon one task to start another. This lack of decisiveness leads to an endless cycle of incomplete efforts. But once you learn to make firm decisions, your work will definitely get completed.

Let's explore some key points that can help in making better decisions and staying committed to your goals.

How to Make the Right Decisions

"Every new idea seems crazy at first."

– Alfred North Whitehead

Making decisions in anger or excitement often leads to regret. The best decisions are made when the mind is calm and composed. Here are some key principles to help you make the right choices:

1. **Identify Your Passion** – Find the field that excites you the most and commit to it wholeheartedly. Whether it's teaching, joining the military, becoming a doctor, playing sports, starting a business, acting, or music pick what truly interests you. Just like a teacher guides students, a soldier protects the nation, and a doctor heals people, your work should add value to society while fulfilling your purpose.

2. **Remove Obstacles** – Before making a decision, analyse potential challenges. If something might distract or block your progress, address it first. A focused mind leads to better execution.

3. **Think Positively** – Your decision should always lead you toward growth and improvement. Avoid choices driven by fear, doubt, or social pressure.

4. **Seek Guidance** – If you're unsure, consult experts in the field. Learning from their experiences can help you make an informed choice.

5. **Believe in Yourself** – Self-confidence is a key factor . Tell yourself that I can and will succeed in this field. A strong belief in your ability will push you through challenges.

6. **Trust the Process** – Be grateful and believe that the universe (or God) supports your journey. This mindset builds unwavering determination.
7. **Surround Yourself with Experts** – Spend time with people who are already successful in your chosen field. Their knowledge and experience will provide valuable insights.
8. **Value Time** – Time is more precious than money. Make sure every decision considers time management, ensuring efficiency and productivity.
9. **Write Down Your Goals** – Put your decision on paper and keep it with you. Review it frequently to stay motivated and focused.
10. **Immerse Yourself in Your Goal** – Read, watch, discuss, and learn everything related to your chosen field. Let curiosity and passion drive you.
11. **Take Action Immediately** – Once you've made a decision, commit to it. Don't wait for the perfect moment start now.
12. **Stay Committed** – Focus on one goal at a time. Avoid distractions or switching between tasks before completing your primary objective.

By following these steps, you will develop clarity, confidence, and discipline in making and achieving your life decisions.

What Should Be the True Goal of Life?

Have you ever thought about what the real purpose of life is? Why is having a life goal important? Is the goal you have set for yourself truly your life's purpose? If not, then what should be the real goal of life?

Most people believe that achieving a good job, becoming a successful entrepreneur, scoring high in exams, or acquiring valuable possessions defines their life's goal. But is that really the ultimate purpose of life? Not at all.

Imagine you set a goal and achieve it within a certain time frame. Can this be considered your life's ultimate purpose? Definitely not. Basic needs like food, clothing, and shelter have always been essential, and even if you fulfil them, human desires never end; they only increase over time.

When I discuss life's purpose with people, they often mention small achievements or material gains. Some say their goal is to be happy. But when I ask how they seek happiness, their answer is often about purchasing things believing that a bigger house, an expensive car, or becoming a company owner will make them happy. But does that truly bring lasting happiness?

Material possessions can provide temporary joy, but they do not lead to lifelong fulfilment. They merely satisfy needs for a short time. The real goal of life should be something that gives you lasting inner peace and contentment.

What Is the True Purpose of Life?

The true purpose of life is to connect with the divine power that sustains our existence. It means:

- **Contemplating the higher purpose** of life beyond daily routines.
- **Remembering and meditating on God** daily, spending at least one or two hours in prayer or self-reflection.
- **Starting every task with gratitude** and seeing God as the centre of all your activities.

- **Experiencing divine love**, which brings unparalleled inner peace and joy.

By doing this, life transforms in an extraordinary way. You will feel a deep sense of happiness that no material possession can provide. Your days will be filled with enthusiasm, positivity, and joy just like celebrating a festival every day.

The ultimate goal of life is not just to survive or accumulate wealth but to live with spiritual awareness and inner fulfilment.

<u>Summary</u>

1. We have two types of Goals in Life– The first is a short-term goal that can be achieved in a limited time. The second and most important goal is attaining God's love, which requires lifelong dedication. This is the true purpose of life.

2. Focused Mindset – See, listen, think, and talk only about what aligns with your chosen goal. Avoid distractions.

3. Commitment to Your Decision – Once you make a decision, stick to it until it is fully accomplished. Do not get involved in other tasks that divert your focus.

4. Observe with a Calm Mind – When analyzing anything, quiet your restless mind using wisdom. This will increase your chances of achieving your goal.

5. True Determination – Real determination means having no alternative options. Stay firm in your resolve.

Chapter 5
Utility of time

"Being busy is not enough. Ants are busy too. The question is: What are you busy with?"

—Henry David Thoreau

Think as big as you want and start moving in that direction. Otherwise, time will pass, and you'll get so caught up in small tasks that you'll never have the chance to think big. Your own small-minded thoughts will already have limited your potential.

Remember your school days? You had to reach school on time. Each subject had a fixed period, school ended at a specific time, you used to reach home play, and go to bed on time. The same routine repeated daily. Eventually, school ended, and you moved on to college, choosing your own path of study. By this point, you started understanding time, but some crucial questions remain:

- "What is the relationship between time and life?" "Do we really feel that time is moving faster than before?" we know that everything changing rapidly, Are we truly making the best use of time in our lives? If not, why? Why is time considered valuable in our lives? What is the connection between time, nature, and human beings? Do we genuinely respect and value time? Why does the same time frame lead some people to success while others remain stuck? How is the modern world introducing new innovations each day with time? Why do most people struggle to complete tasks on time?

Let's try to find answers to these questions. Imagine for a moment if you had always made the right decisions at the right time, how would your life be today? You would probably face far fewer challenges than you do now.

Although everyone tries to complete tasks on time, only a few truly succeed. Now, you might wonder: What is the "right task" and the "right time"? Those who align their actions with time, pursuing a field they are passionate about, and whose work benefits not only themselves but also others these are the ones who achieve true success. Their work is not just for personal gain but is also inspired by the desire to contribute to society.

Understanding the Mathematics of Life

Every person reaches a stage in life where his ability to think and understand begins to awaken. This usually starts around the age of 14 or 15. Understanding the mathematics of time in life is crucial. Those who grasp this concept align their lives accordingly and move in the right direction with time. However, such people are rare. It is essential for everyone, especially students, to be aware of this fact. The longer a person takes to understand and accept the mathematics of life, the more challenging and struggle- filled their journey becomes.

When I was in college, I realized the significance of this life equation. Certain difficulties forced me to pay attention to it, but once I understood the direction of my life and the principles of time, I started moving forward accordingly. As a result, I began to see positive outcomes.

In the beginning, people usually have to work harder. If you experience changes in your daily life, don't be afraid–because change is a law of nature. Nothing on this earth is permanent.

Learning means understanding and applying knowledge in life. However, most of the time, we don't even know why or what we should be learning. When we get bored of studying certain subjects, we often stop reading them altogether. By the age of **24** or **25**, most people enter a job based on their degree level.

A human lifespan is typically considered to be around **100 years.** However, in reality, people rarely live that long. By the age of **60**, most individuals suffer from some serious illness, and many pass away before reaching **70**. Only a small number of people live to be **100 years** old.

Now, let's talk about the mathematics of life. Imagine that a person's lifespan is not **60 or 80,** but **100 years**. Have you ever taken a moment to sit in solitude and calculate your lifespan in terms of hours? Have you ever created a time schedule for your daily activities? Most people would say, "I'm too busy for that, because they are trapped in their own self-created cycle of work.

You may have heard the joke: "I want to cook Halwa (a sweet dish), but I sit inside the pan." If you try making Halwa this way, what will happen? Not only will the dish be cooked, but you will also end up burning yourself ! This is exactly the mistake people make in life.

The simple solution Is to step out of the pan and cook the Halwa properly only then can you enjoy its sweetness. In other words, once we understand our total lifespan, we can avoid wasting time on unimportant things.

God has given everyone the same **24 hours** in a day no more, no less. If we assume a lifespan of 100 years, have you ever calculated the total number of hours in it? We can analyse this with the table of numbers in section **0.04.**

1 Day = 24 hours

12 Months = 365 Or Days (Leap Year)
Total number of hours in 365 days=

365*24= 8760 hours

That is, total number of hours in the year

8760 hours thus , total number of days in

a year = 365 * 100 = 36500 days

So the total number of hours in 100 years= 36500* 24= 876000 hours

Table 0.04

The Value of Time in Life

Right now, as you are reading this book, your age is likely between **15 and 30 years.** However, for an average estimate, let's assume you are **20 years** old. This means that **20 years** of your life have already passed. Have you ever wondered how these **20 years** went by so quickly? No matter how hard you try, you cannot bring back this lost time.

Now, let's analyse how you use the **24 hours** in a day. To understand this better, we divide a day into three parts:

8 + 8 + 8 = 24 hours

Looking at an entire lifespan, we can categorize sleep patterns into different stages: childhood, youth, and old age. Generally, people sleep more during childhood, slightly less in youth, and then either more or less in old age. On an average, a person sleeps for seven hours and twenty minutes every day let's assume about **8 hours a day**, which means that in a lifetime of **100** years **(or 876,000 hours,** as seen in Table **0.04)**, **292,000 hours** are spent sleeping–that's **one-third of their entire life**!

Now, this leaves us with **584,000 hours.** If we look at the second set of **8 hours**, this time is usually dedicated to work whether it's a job, business, or any productive activity. A dedicated and hardworking person spends about **292,000 hours** working over a lifetime.

After sleep and work, the remaining **292,000 hours** (which equals

12,167 days or about **33 years**) are left for everything else. Now, let's examine how we spend the final set of **8 hours:**

Daily Essential Activities

(A) Time spent on eating meals **(3 times a day)**: 30 + 30 + 30 = **90 minutes**

(B) Time spent brushing teeth: **3 minutes**

(C) Time spent on bathing and using the restroom: **45 minutes**

(D) Time spent looking in the mirror: **6 minutes**

These basic activities take a total of **144 minutes** per day **(or 2 hours 24 minutes)**, Over a lifetime of **12,167** days this adds up to **29,200.8** hours

Time Left for Personal Growth and Other Activities

After accounting for sleep, work, and daily activities **(A, B, C, and D)**, the remaining time in life is:

292,000 hours – 29,200.8 hours = 262,799.2 hours

When converted into days and years:

262,799.2 ÷ =24 10,949.96 days

10,949.96 ÷ 365 = approximately **30 years**

So, after all necessary activities, you have **only 30** years left for yourself.

This realization would help you rethink how you use your time. Do you want to continue wasting it, or will you invest it wisely in learning, personal growth, and meaningful experiences?

Understanding the Reality of Time in Life

No human has ever remained completely healthy for a full **100 years.** As we grow up, our body undergoes changes every five years. For example, when a baby's teeth start coming in, they often experience digestive issues. Similarly, despite our constant efforts to maintain good health, imbalances in the body are inevitable. At times, we may even be bedridden for days due to illness.

By now, you have understood the concept of time in life and realized how little time is actually available for truly living. According to this calculation, we effectively get only **30 years** to live. But wait there's more to consider.

These calculations assume a **100-year** lifespan, but if we analyse it further, we realize that the first **10 years** of childhood and the last **10 years** of old age are often spent in dependency or illness. So, out of the **30 years** we have only **two decades** are actually productive.

Now, consider your current age. If you are **20 years** old, then subtracting it from the remaining 30 years leaves you with just **10** productive years.

Sounds shocking, doesn't it? This is the reality of time in life. About **95%** of people live without realizing this truth. They continue following outdated routines, beliefs, and habits without ever questioning them. But time is invaluable–once lost, it can never be regained.

Now that you understand the real value of time, will you continue living the same way, or will you change your mindset and make every moment count? Your mind has the power to achieve whatever you can imagine. If you strengthen your thoughts with determination and strong willpower, you can shape your life the way you truly desire.

I still remember an incident when I had to travel from New Delhi to Gujarat for an interview. My train was scheduled to leave in the evening at a fixed time. Unfortunately, I was just one minute late. As soon as I reached the platform, the train had already started moving.

Though the train wasn't moving very fast, I had to run at full speed to catch it. It was challenging because the platform surface was quite slippery, and there was a risk of falling. But somehow, with great effort, I managed to board the train, found my seat, and took a deep breath of relief. I thanked God if I had been just one more minute late, I would have missed the train.

That incident taught me a valuable lesson. Since then, I have never been late for anything important in life. Whenever I have to go somewhere, I plan everything in advance to ensure I am always on time.

The key takeaway Is that we often realize the importance of time only after it has slipped away. When we miss an opportunity due to a lack of time management, we deeply regret it. But by valuing time and preparing ahead, we can ensure that such regrets never happen again.

Why Do We Waste Time?

Every person has a limited amount of time in life. We all know this, yet we often spend our time on activities that have no real connection to our goals. Instead of focusing on what truly matters, we waste time on things that don't contribute to our growth or success.

One of the biggest distractions today is social media. Even children now spend hours glued to their screens, and for young adults, it's even worse. Many people spend countless hours watching news channels, movies, or debating over political issues. They argue about what a leader should or shouldn't do, criticize policies, and discuss matters that are completely beyond their control.

Take a moment to think will your discussions and debates change anything? No! The real work is being done by those in action, not by those who just talk.

When I interact with young adults, especially those over **24 years** old, I notice a common pattern they often blame others for their failures. They say, "There are no jobs. The government isn't providing opportunities. I have a degree, but I still don't have employment."

But the real question is: Did you truly prepare yourself for success? Did you use those 24 years wisely to develop the right skills? Or did you spend most of your time seeking entertainment and distractions? If you wasted time back then, you can't blame anyone else for your struggles now.

Nothing happens in this world without a reason. Have you ever considered the real purpose of your time? Only a few people truly understand how and where they should invest their time.

The desire for a meaningful life comes from our thoughts, and our thoughts are shaped by our imagination. Everything that exists in the world today every invention, discovery, and progress–was first imagined by someone. Here's something surprising: It takes the same amount of time to think big as it does to think small. Yet, most people choose to think small and limit themselves to a narrow vision of life.

So, the question is : Are you using your time to think big and take meaningful action, or are you just letting it slip away?

Why Laziness?

"Living in laziness is like committing slow suicide."

–Socrates

Laziness is the biggest enemy of success and one of the main reasons people waste time. The best way to overcome laziness is to develop such strong desires for your goals that even the thought of procrastination feels tiring.

Laziness means avoiding work or delaying tasks even when we have the ability to do them. Sometimes, people even refuse to do small tasks at home, like bringing a glass of water for someone. This kind of behaviour weakens discipline and self-respect.

Of course, resting in bed feels good. Many people dream about having everything done for them without moving a muscle. But ask yourself: Is this really how you want to live?

A Look at the Past

Centuries ago, when there were no modern conveniences, people had to do everything themselves:

- Ploughing fields by hand
- Grinding wheat into flour using stone mills
- Cooking food with firewood
- Carrying water from distant wells

Despite such hard work, they remained healthy and happy. Why? Because they had a reason to work if they didn't, they wouldn't survive.

The Present Reality

Today, we have machines and technology to do most of our work. With just a few taps on our phones, we can:

- Order food
- Pay bills
- Get groceries delivered

While technology makes life easier, it also makes people lazy. If we continue to avoid small efforts, laziness will take control of our lives.

The question is: Will you let laziness steal your potential, or will you take control of your time and energy?

Today, we don't need to work as hard as our ancestors did. With modern technology, daily tasks have become much easier. But have we ever thought about how much effort our parents and grandparents put in to provide us with a comfortable life?

Did we ever ask them:

- What struggles did you face to build this home?
- How hard was it to earn a living back then?

Most of us have become dependent on their efforts without realizing our own responsibilities. Instead of just enjoying what they built, we should think about how to expand and improve it for future generations.

If we keep sitting idle, everything they worked for could disappear one day.

Our ancestors had fewer resources but worked tirelessly to achieve their goals. Today, we have all the resources, but we are getting trapped in the comfort zone.

For example:

- Instead of waking up early to do laundry, we think, "I have a washing machine; I can do it later." - Instead of using our free time productively, we waste hours on social media.

Technology is not the problem it helps us save time and energy. The real question is: How are we using the time we save?

What Successful People Do Differently

When I studied the habits of successful people, I found one common trait they wake up early and follow a disciplined routine.

One book that inspired me was "The Miracle Morning" by Hal Elrod. It teaches how to:

- Wake up early

- Start the day with energy up
- Use time wisely

Think about it on the days you wake up early, don't you feel more energetic and happy?

Imagine stepping outside in the morning, feeling the fresh air, listening to the birds chirping, and embracing the gift of nature.

Would you really want to miss out on this beautiful experience every day?

Everyone would love to receive such a beautiful gift from nature. The day I experienced this gift and understood the value of time in life, I decided to wake up early every morning with a clear goal in mind. Since then, I have been waking up early every day and consider this habit a blessing in my life. I express my gratitude to God daily for this special gift.

The most joyful part of my 24-hour day is the first three hours of the morning. During that time, there is such a deep sense of peace in the world, and the gentle morning breeze feels as if the flowers and leaves in the garden are talking to me. Moments like these are too precious to miss.

If you truly want to live life to the fullest, take a pledge today to wake up early. Do not let laziness, the enemy of progress, waste your valuable time—defeat it every day. In the beginning, waking up early may feel difficult, but no good habit is formed instantly. It requires practice, and we practice only when we have a strong desire to learn and grow.

If there is one thing in this world that can truly be stolen, it is time. You might wonder how can time be stolen? The answer lies in understanding the value of time and using it wisely.

Since time is limited, it should be used only for achieving your goals and nothing else.

For example, if you have a habit of sleeping during the day, listening to too much music, playing excessively, or spending hours chatting with people, it doesn't mean you have to stop these activities completely. Playing is good for your health, but you should set a specific time for it. Similarly, when traveling, instead of wasting hours watching movies or engaging in pointless conversations, you can make better use of this time by reading an inspiring book that helps you stay motivated and focused on your goals.

Many people sleep at night but also take long naps during the day, which is not a good habit. A short rest of 45 minutes to an hour is fine, but no more than that. Try to sleep early at night so you can wake up early and be productive.

When attending weddings or celebrations, staying up late can disrupt your schedule for the next few days. If you frequently attend such events, you will lose a lot of valuable time. Weddings and celebrations will always happen, but your primary focus should be on achieving your goals. First, accomplish what you are working hard for your studies, learning new skills, and gaining experience. Once you reach your goals, you can give attention to other things.

Throughout life, there will be many distractions–small tasks and events that have no connection to your goals. You must be mindful and consciously avoid these distractions. Instead, focus on the activities that truly matter and contribute to your success.

When you do any task in your daily routine, do you always complete it within a fixed time? Probably not you might take a little longer than planned. For example, when appearing for competitive or academic exams after college or graduation, you are given a fixed time limit to answer all the questions. Initially, when you receive the question paper, you might feel that two or three hours are enough. However, once you start writing, only a few students manage to complete the exam on time, while others feel that time is running out. Even if they know the answers, they struggle to write them within the given time. This happens to many students.

Similarly, in daily life, most people struggle to complete tasks within a fixed time. Some activities, like getting ready for work on time, going to school or college, and eating meals at the right time, are usually done on schedule. However, what about other tasks? Do you sleep and wake up at a fixed time? Do you maintain a routine for personal hygiene like bathing and other morning activities? While you do these things daily, you may not have set a proper time for them.

Now, think for a moment why haven't you set a specific time for these small tasks? If you want to achieve something big in life, can you do it within a fixed timeframe? No! If you cannot manage small tasks within a set time, how can you expect to complete big tasks on time? This is the main reason why people often achieve their goals much later than planned something they aimed to accomplish by 30 might take until 40 or 50, or sometimes, they never achieve it at all. Most people want to do a lot in life, but only those succeed who follow proper time management, even for the smallest tasks. If you aim for big achievements but struggle to accomplish them, the key is to manage your time efficiently from small tasks to big projects.

Look at birds they chirp at a fixed time every morning and return to their nests at a fixed time in the evening. Even nature follows a schedule seasons change at specific intervals, and fruits ripen at the right time. Everything in nature follows a set cycle.

When you start working on something, you might stay focused initially, but after a while, distractions take over, causing delays. So how can you ensure that you complete tasks on time? Let's understand this better.

Pomodoro Technique

The Pomodoro Technique was developed by Francesco Cirillo in the late 1980s. It is a time management method inspired by Japanese techniques. This method helps in completing tasks efficiently within a set time frame.

Often, when we start working on something, we are highly focused at first, but after some time, our concentration weakens. As a result, tasks take longer to complete, and mistakes happen. This is common not only in studying but in almost every field. Scientific research shows that after a certain period, the brain gets tired, muscles become weak, and our mind needs rest.

What is the Pomodoro Technique?

Let's understand it step by step:

25 minutes of focused work + 5 minutes of complete rest- Choose a task and work on it with full concentration for 25 minutes. During this time, avoid all distractions no checking phones, no unnecessary breaks, and no shifting focus. - After 25 minutes, take a 5-minute break not for scrolling social media or walking around but for complete mental relaxation.

- One session consists of 4 Pomodoros - Work 25 minutes, then take a 5-minute break (this is one Pomodoro).- Repeat this cycle four times (100 minutes total). After four Pomodoros, take a longer break of 15–30 minutes to refresh your mind.

This technique has proven to be highly effective. Whenever I need to learn something new, memorize a speech, or prepare for an event, I use this method. Before discovering Pomodoro, I often struggled to complete tasks on time. However, using this technique has helped me manage my time better and stay energized throughout my work.

Summary

1. Time is the most valuable resource in life. Everyone should learn to "steal" time from distractions and use it wisely.
2. Dedicate at least three hours every morning to yourself before starting your day. This helps in self-growth and productivity.
3. Laziness is the enemy of success. It shows a lack of understanding of time's value. Consider laziness as your biggest obstacle and strive to overcome it daily.
4. Plan your free time wisely. After sleeping and working, manage the remaining hours by making a task list. This will benefit you in the long run.
5. Use the Pomodoro Technique to stay focused and complete tasks efficiently within a fixed time.

Chapter 6

A Better Attempt at Understanding Yourself

"To know yourself, think about yourself."

– Socrates

You are the only one who can play your role in this world.

No one else on this planet can live your life or be you.

We can truly understand ourselves only when we stop trying to understand others. However, we have a long-standing habit of constantly analysing and judging others. Instead of looking outward, we need to look within.

Unfortunately, people today are more interested in discussing others rather than reflecting on themselves. Even though we may have countless flaws, we rarely notice them. Instead, we focus only on the faults and shortcomings of others because we are always peering into their lives.

Let's consider a few key points:

1. Every person on this earth is unique in terms of appearance, shape, and way of thinking. However, physically, we all have the same basic structure two hands, two legs, two eyes, two ears, and the same sensory organs. The only real difference is in our mindset. No one is born with all knowledge and abilities; they have to acquire them over time. For example, when a baby is born, it has no teeth and no understanding of language. Teeth

grow later, and the child learns the language and culture of the environment in which he is raised.

2. A person's success in life depends on the development of their intelligence and awareness. The truth is that everyone has the potential to grow intellectually as much as they wish. The more one cultivates their mind, the more successful and capable they become.

Do you know the worth of a healthy body? You might think this is a strange question and say, "It's priceless!"

Once, in the United States, a group of scientists attempted to create a human body in a laboratory not a living one, but a replica of a deceased body. After several experiments, they estimated that constructing such a body would cost around five trillion dollars.

However, even if they managed to create this body, it wouldn't be able to laugh when praised, get angry when insulted, or feel hungry when delicious food was placed before it. Now, think about this if a lifeless human body is worth five trillion dollars, can we even measure the value of a living human body?

Just imagine you carry this immense wealth with you every single moment whether you're awake, asleep, or going about your day. It is said that the human brain is like an entire continent in itself. Yet, the biggest mystery is that we fail to recognize and utilize this incredible gift. We are so caught up in small, insignificant matters that we don't even realize the true power we carry within us.

There are nearly eight billion people on this planet, and many of them were born with disabilities or faced life-altering accidents. Yet, they chose to live life beautifully and achieved remarkable things. Some of these inspirational figures include:

Nick Vujicic, Arunima Sinha, Stephen Hawking, Sudha Chandran Sadhana Dhawan, Ravindra Jain, H. Ramakrishnan, Sam Cawthorn, Rajendra Singh Rahelu

Despite their physical limitations, they never let themselves feel handicapped. They embraced life, understood its true value, and made the most of it. Now, if they could achieve so much with fewer abilities, imagine what we who have even more capabilities can accomplish!

Every person possesses a unique and special talent that sets them apart from others. Those who take the time to discover their talent eventually find it. For instance, some people have a melodious voice, some enjoy public speaking, while others excel in acting, sports, or playing musical instruments. The ones who identify their strengths, focus on them, and move forward with dedication often achieve their desired success in life. On the other hand, some people keep wandering in circles, unable to make the most of their potential.

Imagine a flute player who roams around the streets of a village, carrying multiple flutes and playing a sweet tune to attract buyers. His life revolves around selling flutes, and he continues this cycle without significant progress. Meanwhile, another person who also plays the flute decides to make it his life's profession. He recognizes his talent, believes in himself, and strengthens his determination. With persistent practice and unwavering confidence, he rises above the ordinary.

One day, this dedicated flute player finds himself performing alongside great musicians, leaving a lasting impression on people's hearts wherever he goes. What once seemed impossible for an ordinary person becomes his reality. Today, he is counted among successful individuals, solely because of his passion for playing the flute. More importantly, he is happy and content with his work.

This example highlights a crucial lesson: one flute player spends his entire life wandering from village to village, merely selling flutes, while another turns his flute-playing into a profession, practices diligently, and achieves success at a young age. The difference lies not in talent, but in recognizing it, believing in it, and taking action to refine and pursue it.

Every person has a unique talent hidden within them. However, until we look within ourselves to discover it and bring it out, we continue to wander aimlessly.

It Is often heard in middle-class or lower-income families that when a child talks about achieving something big in life or becoming a successful person, instead of encouraging them, most family members mock them. They say things like, "No one in our family has ever become successful, so how can you?" Hearing this, the child becomes disheartened and starts believing that they can never achieve greatness.

This kind of limited thinking creates a mental barrier in the child's mind, and they begin to accept it as the truth. As they grow up, they continue to think within these restrictions and shape their life accordingly. Eventually, they spend their entire life like a frog in a well, never realizing their full potential.

Every student reads many books throughout their life. But do they truly read for themselves? No. In reality, most of these books are only studied to pass exams, and once the exams are over, their knowledge is forgotten. Now, think about it–if the education from these books cannot support us throughout our lives, how much value do they actually hold? The key is to read more books that provide lifelong wisdom and guidance, rather than just those that help us pass exams.

Making Excuses

You might remember how, as a child you sometimes didn't feel like going to school. And when you returned after two or three days, the teacher would make you stand up in class and ask, "Why didn't you come to school?"

But you were smart you had already planned your answer. Without hesitation, you would make up an excuse, like having a stomach-ache or something else. Sometimes, you managed to fool the teacher, but when they spoke to your parents, your lie would be exposed.

From childhood, you learned to make excuses sometimes to avoid studying, sometimes to escape other responsibilities. Over time, this habit became so deeply ingrained in your subconscious mind that even today, you continue to make excuses. The only difference is that the reasons have changed. As a child, you made excuses to have fun; now, you make excuses to avoid hard work.

People often say things like:

- "I can't do this task. "I don't have enough money to start this work."

Most people use such excuses to avoid challenges. However, those who are determined to achieve something in life always find opportunities instead of excuses. They never shy away from difficulties. Even if they have to put in extra effort in the beginning, they don't mind because they believe that tomorrow will be better than today. With this mindset, they keep moving forward.

The small habits we develop in life eventually shape our future. Whether good or bad, they become a visible part of our behaviour and influence our success.

Observing Your Own Work

Observation means carefully noticing and understanding things. In our daily lives, many events happen, and we perform countless actions, but how often do we truly pay attention to them?

For example:

- When we brush our teeth, do we know how many strokes it takes to clean them properly?
- When we eat a piece of bread, do we notice how many bites it takes to finish it?
- How many times do we chew our food before swallowing?
- When we use an object and put it back, do we handle it with care and respect?
- Have we ever observed the way we walk?
- What kind of words do we use when talking to others?
- How do our thoughts affect our emotions?
- After a conversation, how does the other person react to us?
- How do we sit while eating?
- What is our sleeping posture?
- What is the first thing we do after waking up in the morning?

There are hundreds of such questions that we may have never thought about. This means we have never truly observed our own actions. If we had, we could have avoided many small mistakes in life.

(Note: Try this once for yourself)

When I started observing both small and big events in my life, I noticed hundreds of mistakes that I had been making unconsciously. Then, I worked on correcting them one by one. Over time, these mistakes reduced significantly.

When we start observing small things, the big things automatically start improving. Carefully analysing our actions helps us do things better the next time. Observation is the key to continuous self-improvement.

Interest means having enthusiasm or curiosity for doing something, or in simple words, not getting bored easily while doing a task.

It is not necessary for a person to follow the same profession as their father or ancestors. Every individual has their own unique interests because not everyone likes the same things. Some people enjoy eating mangoes, while others prefer bananas or different fruits. Similarly, when it comes to choosing a career or activity, everyone has their own preferences, which cannot be forced to change. However, we can modify how we approach or do things.

The same difference is seen in sports some people like cricket, others prefer hockey, badminton, or different games. In the music world, not everyone can become Lata Mangeshkar, in cricket, not everyone can be Sachin Tendulkar, and in acting not everyone can be Arun Govil or Amitabh Bachchan. Every person has its own unique qualities and strengths.

Only we know what we are truly curious and passionate about.

People naturally prefer doing things they are interested in. I have seen many students who, when choosing subjects for further studies, simply follow their friends' choices even if they have no real interest in that field. As a result, they struggle and fail to succeed in the long run.

This happens because they make decisions based on others rather than their own interests. When someone chooses a career just by copying others, they often find themselves unhappy and unsuccessful. On the other hand, a wise person tries to master the field they are genuinely interested in because they understand that the secret to success lies in pursuing their true passion.

Note: What are your true interests? Identify five areas where you believe you can perform your best. Write them down and reflect on them.

Success is already within you just need to recognize and bring it out!

Activity:

1. ______________________________

2. ______________________________

3. ______________________________

4. ______________________________

5. ______________________________

Good and Bad Habits

Every person has two types of habits: good habits and bad habits. However, bad habits usually develop more easily than good ones. Good habits require conscious effort to build, while bad habits tend to form on their own.

Have you ever taken the time to identify your positive qualities the ones that help you become a better person? Also, can you list ten good habits that you follow every day? And most importantly, are you able to add one new good habit to your daily routine regularly?

I personally started adding one new good habit to my routine every day, and over time, I saw a significant improvement in my overall behaviour and lifestyle.

Example:

Waking up late in the morning is a bad habit that many people want to change. Suppose you usually wake up at 8 AM, but you want to start waking up at 5 AM. You might manage to wake up early for a day or two, but since your body is used to 8 AM, you will likely fall back into your old habit.

To change this, follow a step-by-step approach:

1. First, start going to bed at a fixed time every night.
2. Instead of suddenly shifting to 5 AM, gradually adjust your wake-up time. Begin by waking up 15 minutes earlier every few days.
3. Write down your new wake-up time on paper. If you wake up at 8 AM, set a goal to wake up at 7:45 AM and write it down. Before sleeping, look at this time and remind yourself that you need to wake up at 7:45 AM.
4. Follow this routine for two to three weeks. Once your body adjusts, reduce your wake-up time by another 15 minutes (7:30 AM) and repeat the process.

5. Keep making gradual adjustments until you reach your desired wake-up time. Eventually, waking up early will become a natural part of your daily routine.

This method can be applied to changing any habit. If you genuinely want to get rid of your bad habits, follow this system consistently, and you will see a transformation.

Action Plan:

1. Follow this process honestly if you miss a day, restart from the beginning.
2. Write down the habits you want to change.
3. Keep reviewing your list throughout the day and remind yourself that you must eliminate these bad habits.
4. Stick to any new habit for at least 2-3 weeks before making further changes.

By following this simple yet effective approach, you can gradually replace bad habits with good ones and improve your Life.

Once you follow this process, you will notice a positive change in your life. Your list of good habits will grow, and over time, something even more surprising will happen your entire life will transform. The things that once held you back will no longer exist, because good habits naturally lead to better results.

Attitude

-A poet has beautifully expressed the power of attitude in these four lines:

- "Change your thoughts, and the destiny will change.
- Change your vision, and the views will change.

- Switching boats won't help much Change your direction, and the shore will change."

Everyone enjoys watching movies in theatres. The first time I visited a cinema hall, I was given a pair of 3D glasses. I had never worn such glasses before.

Before the movie started, all the lights in the hall were switched off, except for the screen's glow. The darkness felt a little scary at first, but I was sitting with my friend in the last row, at the top. It was our first time in a theatre.

The movie began. As the scenes played out before my eyes, I felt as if I was a part of the film itself. During funny moments, I couldn't stop laughing, and I felt deeply connected to the humour.

Then, a scene came where the hero was being attacked by goons, and his family was being treated cruelly. I felt an unexpected pain in my heart how could this happen? My eyes were lost in that world, and I had no control over what I was seeing and hearing.

I looked around and saw that everyone was feeling the same emotions some looked sad, while others even had tears in their eyes. At that moment, I realized something powerful: none of this was real, yet our emotions reacted as if it was real.

Suddenly, the scene changed. A new wave of energy filled the air, and the emotions shifted. How strange that our eyes can make us laugh, cry, or feel deep sorrow in just a few moments

This experience made me question: Why are our emotions so weak that we believe in something that isn't even real? Why is our perspective so fragile that it can't even distinguish between truth and fiction?

The answer lies in the fact that most of us are unaware of what truly shapes our lives. When I studied the lives of successful people, I discovered that their perspective is very different from the average person. Their emotions are not weak; they are strong and resilient.

They don't just see things at a surface level they observe deeply, from the root to the peak, before reacting emotionally. Their long- term vision helps them navigate life with clarity and wisdom. Have we ever thought about seeing the world from a deeper perspective? To truly understand attitude, we must not just look at things superficially. Instead, we should step back and develop the ability to see both the inner and outer aspects of a situation.

When we don't fully understand something, it affects us emotionally, often in a way that can be dangerous. That's why it is important to understand anything properly before we see, hear, or act upon it. Otherwise, we might get trapped in a situation that is as difficult as being lost in the ocean where even if we try to swim out, we can't escape. It wouldn't just be hard, but almost impossible.

Everything that exists in this world today began as a simple imagination. Our thoughts shape our reality whatever we imagine becomes the foundation for our beliefs. If our thoughts are positive or negative, their depth and intensity influence our perspective and actions. Ultimately, our way of thinking determines the kind of life we create for ourselves.

Dreams of Life

If our dreams are small, the world seems small to us. But if our dreams are big, the same world appears vast and full of possibilities. Every person dreams there's nothing wrong with dreaming. In fact, everyone holds on to some dream or another in life. But here's something interesting: when we dream at night, and when we live through a day, both eventually pass and become the past.

If we call the past a dream, it wouldn't be wrong. The truth is, the dreams we see in sleep are not the real dreams of life. A real dream is one that, even after we are gone, continues to inspire and guide others for generations.

Many people see dreams but never fulfil them. Their dreams last only for a moment like closing and opening their eyes and eventually, their precious life slips away without those dreams becoming a reality. Dreams should not just be dreams; they should turn into missions.

The real problem arises when we keep thinking about the past or worrying about the future, while forgetting to live in the present but past, present, and future are all deeply connected. Our present is the result of our past actions, and the future will be shaped by what we do today. So instead of regretting the past, we should learn from it and focus on taking the right actions in the present so that our future becomes bright and successful.

Summary

1. Focus on Yourself – When you stop thinking about others and start focusing on yourself, studying your own thoughts and actions, life begins to move closer to reality.

2. Self-Acceptance is Key – You cannot move forward in life until you accept yourself as you truly are.

3. Elevate Your Perspective – The bigger the goal, the higher and more positive your mindset needs to be.

4. Control Over Emotions Leads to Greatness - When a person gains control over their emotions, they can achieve extraordinary things in life.
5. Live in the Present - Learn from the past and keep the future in mind, but don't get stuck regretting the past or worrying about the future. Focus on making the present moment meaningful.
6. Good Habits Take Time - Bad habits develop quickly, but good habits take effort and patience to build.

Chapter 7
How to Elevate and Strengthen Your Thoughts

"Think twice before you speak, because your words and their impact can plant the seeds of success or failure in others' minds."

– Napoleon Hill

Indian civilization and culture have a unique and prominent place in the world. Each state in India is known for its diverse traditions and sacred sites. I feel proud to have been born in this great land. Learning about Indian culture and experiencing the beauty of nature watching birds soar in the sky, listening to humming bees, and admiring blooming flowers in lush green valleys gives me deep inner joy.

I love traveling and cannot stop myself from visiting multiple spiritual places every year. When I started working on myself, life became much easier. Traveling is my passion. So far, I have visited Gujarat, Rajasthan, Punjab, Delhi, Bihar, Odisha, Jharkhand, Uttarakhand, and many other states. I also enjoy walking journeys. Sitting under the shade of roadside trees, chatting with elderly people, brings a different kind of peace. The people living near railway tracks and highways often seem happier than those in urban areas. Talking to them creates a unique sense of connection.

During my travels, I meet people of all kinds, and their conversations always seem interesting. Some people talk a lot, while others speak very little. I have noticed that those who talk excessively without meaningful reasoning are often surrounded by problems and stress. If a person reduces negative speech, many of their problems naturally fade away. Some people provoke us for no reason, and we react instantly. This means someone else is controlling our emotions. Instead of ignoring their words, we feel the need to respond, which only entangles us further.

Today, people are more focused on bringing others down. Such behaviour has increased significantly. In some ways, even herbivorous animals seem kinder than humans. In today's world, we need faith, love, and courage more than ever. Elevating and strengthening our thoughts is not as easy as it seems. A person is identified by their thoughts and words, as speech is one of the most important qualities of a human being. It is said that a fool remains unnoticed until they speak.

The true purpose of education is to refine one's character and make thoughts pure and powerful. Thoughts originate from imagination, and our thinking is influenced by what we see and hear. The kind of words we listen to, the things we focus on, and what we study all shape our thoughts. When we speak, do we pay attention to our words? This is crucial because our thoughts define who we are.

It is said that a fool remains unnoticed until he speaks. The true purpose of education is to refine a person's character and make their thoughts pure and strong. Thoughts originate from imagination, and thinking is shaped by what we see and hear. In our daily lives, the kind of words we listen to, the things we focus on, and what we study all influence our thoughts. But when we speak, do we truly pay attention to our words? This is crucial because our thoughts define who we are.

I still cannot forget this incident it continues to inspire me. Once, during a pilgrimage, I unknowingly wandered into an unfamiliar place. I didn't have much with me just a bag filled with books, along with two or three sets of clothes. The bag weighed around four to five kilograms, and I also carried a bottle of water. It was my first time visiting that place, and the path passed through a village. As I approached the entrance, I saw a strict police presence guarding the area. No one was allowed to enter before 4 AM.

Since it was early morning, some of the officers appeared sleepy, though others remained fully alert at the gate. As soon as I reached them, they stopped me and began searching my belongings. They noticed the books and clothes in my bag. One officer, seeing the books, asked, "Are you a poet?" Hesitantly, I replied, "Yes, I recite poetry." Another officer then said, "Then recite a poem for us." It was 3 AM. I washed my face with water the dust from walking had settled on my skin. Then, I recited two poems in front of them. A slack smile appeared on their faces, and they seemed pleased. Soon after, they permitted me to pass. That day, I truly understood the power of words that travelled from my lips to their ears, carrying meaning and impact. I realized that if one's thoughts are strong and positive, every path in life becomes easier.

All great individuals in history had great thoughts that made them elevate, positive, and strong. In life, we should speak in the same proportion as we listen. However, as humans, we often fail to do so because we do not enjoy listening. More importantly, even when we do listen, the quality of what we hear matters. The kind of thoughts we absorb shapes the kind of thoughts we produce.

Effect of Thoughts in Our Life

In our lives, two types of thoughts continuously influence us: positive thoughts and negative thoughts. The way we think determines our emotions, and we attract experiences that align with our feelings. The universe is filled with both positive and negative thought vibrations, though they are so subtle that they cannot be seen with the naked eye.

You may have noticed that when you feel sad, you often listen to melancholic music. This happens because, at that moment, your emotions are tuned to negativity. It works just like a radio station where various channels are available, and we choose one based on our mood. Similarly, in life, both good and bad thoughts surround us ; it is up to us to decide which ones we allow into our minds. The good news is that, just like changing a radio channel, we can shift our thoughts anytime. When we align ourselves with positive thoughts, we feel happiness, peace, satisfaction, joy, and love, which are the most desirable human experiences.

When I read The Secret by Rhonda Byrne, I realized that thoughts have the power to transform a person completely. We have the ability to take our thinking in any direction we choose, and the most successful people in the world understand this. Once we develop a strong and determined mindset towards achieving something, we eventually attract it into our lives. I have personally witnessed this "secret" working in my life. What we deeply believe and embed in our subconscious mind starts manifesting into reality, and even the universe aligns to help us achieve it. It is astonishing how this happens!

The first time I applied this principle, I was amazed. I kept thinking about how powerful thoughts truly are. Using this knowledge, we can achieve anything happiness, prosperity, wealth, and success all the things people work hard for. However, we also constantly encounter negative thoughts, which often take over when we are emotionally weak. This is especially true when we are idle and not engaged in anything productive.

As the saying goes, "An empty mind is the devil's workshop." To counter negative thoughts, we must keep ourselves occupied with meaningful and purposeful activities that align with our life goals.

Be Aware of Your Thoughts

Before listening to someone else, we must first listen to ourselves. Is the person worth listening to? Are their thoughts meaningful and insightful? If their words lack wisdom and inspiration, we should avoid absorbing them, as negative thoughts can lead us in the wrong direction.

Similarly, when expressing our own thoughts, we must be mindful. If we unintentionally use harsh words, we should immediately apologize. Mistakes happen, but being aware of our thoughts and speech is essential.

"Socrates once said: Be mindful of your words, as they can either lift you up or pull you down."

I've observed that some people are on the verge of great success, but due to careless speech, they end up facing severe consequences. This is why we must always think before we speak.

We live in a society where we encounter many different perspectives. Just like a river naturally flows toward the ocean, our thoughts also flow in a particular direction. It is up to us to ensure that they are moving positively.

The Power and Responsibility of Words

- People often forget that their words can leave a deep impact on others. A good leader, or simply a good person, always chooses words carefully because:
- **Words Reflect Respect** No matter who you are speaking to, if you use respectful language, you will receive respect in return.
- **Words Can Build or Break *Relationships*** A kind word can brighten someone's day, while a harsh word can hurt their self- esteem.
- **Every Person Has Their Own Dignity** Someone who works for you today might be a leader in their own family. Everyone has their struggles and responsibilities, so never underestimate anyone.
- **Words Can Inspire** The right words at the right time can change a person's life. A good leader uses words to uplift and motivate others.

How to Control Your Words ?

Think before you speak – Consider how your words might affect the other person.

Stay calm in anger If you are upset, take a moment to cool down before speaking.

Choose clarity over harshness Speak firmly but respectfully.

Make politeness a habit – Treat everyone with kindness, no matter who they are.

"Even a servant in your house is the master of their own home." This means that every person is important in their own way. No one should be judged only by their current role, as they have their own struggles and responsibilities. Therefore, always speak thoughtfully let your words uplift others instead of making them feel small.

Drive Away Bad Thoughts

When negative thoughts take over, they cloud our judgment and push us toward harmful actions. People trapped in negativity often face constant struggles and difficulties. Even when they try to escape, they remain stuck because they fail to recognize the root cause of their negative thinking.

This is why it is crucial to identify the source of bad thoughts only then can we eliminate them. Just like a doctor diagnoses an illness before prescribing medicine, we must first understand why we are experiencing negative thoughts before we can remove them.

One of the biggest influences on our thoughts is the company we keep. Our surroundings and the people we interact with shape our mindset. If we spend time with positive, purpose-driven individuals who contribute to society, our thoughts naturally improve.

However, even if we have good thoughts, being around the wrong people can negatively influence us. The story of the Mahabharata teaches us an important lesson: We should align ourselves with the righteous Pandavas, guided by Lord Krishna, rather than the Kauravas, who were led astray.

Surrounding ourselves with pure-hearted, wise, and spiritually strong individuals will naturally lead us toward positivity, growth, and success.

In the Ramayana, there is an important episode that shows how a single wrong thought can change circumstances drastically. King Dasharatha had three queens Kaushalya, Kaikeyi, and Sumitra.

He loved all three dearly, and they were all noble-hearted women. His eldest son, Lord Rama, was born to Kaushalya. Kaikeyi, too, loved Rama as her own son.

However, everything changed when Manthara, Kaikeyi's maid, started poisoning her mind. She planted seeds of doubt and jealousy, convincing Kaikeyi that her son Bharata should be crowned king instead of Rama. Under Manthara's influence, Kaikeyi's thoughts turned negative, and she demanded that Rama be exiled to the forest for fourteen years so Bharata could rule Ayodhya.

The consequences of this decision were devastating. King Dasharatha, heartbroken by his son's exile, could not bear the pain and passed away. Meanwhile, Bharata, instead of rejoicing, was furious at his mother for her actions. He refused to sit on the throne and instead ruled Ayodhya for fourteen years using Lord Rama's sandals as a symbol of his rule. Ultimately, Kaikeyi's plan backfired, leaving her with nothing "She lost both her illusion and Lord Rama"

Even in today's society, we come across people like Manthara those who manipulate others for their own gain. Such individuals can influence even the kindest hearts, leading them astray with misleading thoughts. Human nature is flexible, and people can be easily influenced by either good or bad advice. However, if one follows the wrong path, the results can be disastrous.

This teaches us that we must be cautious about the advice we receive and the company we keep. Negative influences can lead to irreversible mistakes, just as they did in the Ramayana.

Summary

1. In this world, you will meet all kinds of people some sweet, some bitter, and some intense. The type of people who come into your life will often reflect the nature of your own thoughts.
2. The true purpose of education is to develop one's character and to cultivate pure and strong thoughts.
3. Bad habits are born from negative thoughts. If we identify their root cause, we can change them easily.
4. A person's thoughts do not become pure and elevated by chance; they are refined through the fire of human values. This is possible for all of us.
5. The right thoughts shape your future life.

Chapter 8
The Art of Conversation

Conversation refers to a formal or informal exchange of words between two or more people with a specific purpose.

When we were children, did we know how to communicate? The answer is 'no'. In childhood, we didn't even know how to speak properly, let alone have conversations. As we all know, communication requires a language so that we can share our thoughts with others and receive a response. When a baby needs something, they use body language or gestures because they cannot speak. They do not know any language yet. For example, when a baby needs something, they start crying, and the mother understands the reason behind it. Sometimes the baby laughs, sometimes they scream, and sometimes they jump with excitement. This means that from birth itself, a child starts communicating through body language.

In fact, a simple smile is often the first step in a conversation. The special thing is that nature has given the gift of smiling only to humans. Have you ever seen an animal's smile? No matter what the situation in life is, we should always keep a smile on our faces. This not only makes us feel positive but also encourages the other person to talk to us in a cheerful manner. India is a country where people often say, "I am very busy," regardless of whether they are actually working or not. However, you will rarely hear anyone say, "I am busy talking."

It has been observed that women tend to engage in conversations more than men. They always have a wide variety of topics to discuss, which is quite fascinating. The reason behind this might be that while men are occupied with work for about eight hours a day, women, especially homemakers, need a way to spend their time. This is why they often engage in conversations and develop a habit of talking.

From small matters to big issues, they discuss topics related to family, relatives, society, and the village. This is a common social pattern, but in reality, many of these conversations may not hold significant importance.

The Importance of Conversation on Different Levels

Even at the international level, India primarily resolves its issues through dialogue. Diplomatic and political relations with other countries are established and maintained through discussions. At the national level, government ministers and administrative officials engage in discussions to make important decisions. The methods of communication may vary at national and international levels.

For example, if a neighbouring country trespasses into Indian territory or makes an unauthorized claim, India first attempts to resolve the issue through dialogue. This shows how crucial the art of conversation is in handling matters at family, social, national, and international levels.

People communicate in different ways, and conversation itself has various forms. Have you ever noticed why a speaker's way of speaking feels different from ours? What makes their speech more impactful?

If you observe a skilled speaker, you'll notice that they express their words clearly and effectively. Think about a news anchor when they speak on television, they don't just use words; they also use body language to convey their message with greater impact.

Similarly, when a well-known journalist interviews a famous personality, the exchange of questions and answers is a perfect example of the highest level of conversational art. The way they structure their words, respond to each other, and maintain the flow of dialogue demonstrates the power of effective communication.

One Language is Essential

I have spent most of my life in Bihar, where people primarily speak Bhojpuri and Hindi. Apart from these languages Maithili, Angika, and Vajjika are also spoken. However, in all schools, Hindi is the primary language for education.

Students spend a few hours at school speaking Hindi, but as soon as they return home, they switch to Bhojpuri. As a result, they neither learn proper Hindi nor fluent Bhojpuri. On top of that, they also have to study Sanskrit and English. English is given more importance after the 10th grade, making the situation even more confusing.

Now, think about it when the education system itself does not focus on mastering a single language, how can a student become proficient in any language? This language confusion creates a lifelong struggle where students fail to gain strong command over any language. But in reality, mastering at least one language is essential in life.

Why Students Struggle with Language?

I have observed that many students focus on learning a new language instead of mastering the one they already know.

For example, in Uttar Pradesh, Bihar, and Jharkhand, where Hindi is the primary language, many students already understand basic

Hindi but struggle to speak it correctly. Instead of improving their Hindi, they focus entirely on learning English and often fail in that too.

In reality, the purpose of any language is simply to express thoughts clearly so that others can understand and respond. Just like water quenches thirst whether it is served in a glass made of glass or steel the function of a language is only to facilitate communication.

Choosing the Right Language for Communication

My native language was Bhojpuri, but I was never able to speak it fluently. At the same time, I also knew some Hindi. When I realized that one language is essential for effective communication, I chose Hindi over Bhojpuri.

Why ? Because Hindi is a more widely spoken language in India, and it is easier for a larger audience to understand. Hindi also felt more natural and useful for me.

However, learning a language in a different environment comes with challenges. If everyone around you speaks Bhojpuri and you start speaking Hindi, people will mock you. This is normal people often resist change. But instead of focusing on their taunts, one should stay focused on learning.

Many people give up because of criticism and remain stuck in life. But those who push forward despite negativity eventually succeed and overcome challenges.

Social Interaction

The way we interact in society is deeply influenced by the values and upbringing we receive in our families. Whether in villages or cities, people's behaviour and communication style reflect their upbringing.

Earlier, in villages, even a small event would bring the entire community together. If a problem arose, people would sit together and find a solution through discussion. Elders shared inspiring stories, and children listened to them with interest. There was a sense of unity and love in interactions.

However, today's situation has changed. Neighbours, once considered family, have now become rivals. Even for a wedding or celebration, we must formally invite our neighbours, who often respond with jealousy rather than joy. Small issues create conflicts and misunderstandings among people. Now, even family members lack mutual respect and affection.

People want to communicate, but instead of bonding with their own family and society, they seek connections elsewhere. This growing division and lack of empathy have weakened social harmony. Society is no longer the same as it was before.

The Decline of Social Values

Disputes over land, property, or minor disagreements have led to people abusing, threatening, and even harming each other. It is shocking to see brothers turning against each other. Life has become so cheap, and people are so caught up in their egos that they fail to realize the damage they are causing.

We often speak about improving our nation, but how can a country change if its people fail to maintain even basic social values? If we cannot communicate respectfully within our own families and communities, talking about national reform is nothing but a delusion.

The Hypocrisy in Social Behaviour

Many people change their tone and behaviour based on where they are.

- In public meetings or panchayat discussions, they act serious and formal. At home, their language and attitude completely change. This is nothing but pretense. If we cannot communicate properly in our families and local communities, how can we expect to behave wisely in larger social settings?

The Impact of Our Words

We must remember that every word we speak returns to us in some way. The small habits and communication patterns we develop in our daily lives eventually influence how we interact socially and professionally.

Once we understand the importance of respectful and meaningful communication, our social interactions will naturally improve. The moment we realize the power of our words, we will start seeing positive changes in our relationships and society.

Charm with Your Words

Have you ever noticed how the receptionist at a hotel or a company speaks? Whether it's a three-star or five-star hotel, the staff welcomes guests politely and warmly. Their way of speaking is pleasant and engaging, making visitors feel comfortable and valued.

Just like that, a person's way of speaking and presenting information can attract others. A friendly and well-mannered conversation creates a positive impression and makes people more interested in what you have to say.

My favourite meal is paalak paneer (spinach with cottage cheese) and rice. While I was in Rajkot city Gujarat, I once visited a hotel with a friend to enjoy my favourite dish on Diwali.

As we entered, we saw a well-dressed young woman at the reception desk. She had a pleasant voice and used body language effectively while speaking. Every guest who entered was greeted warmly, and she enthusiastically described the hotel's best dishes and services.

Her way of talking was so charming that it instantly made us feel comfortable, and we decided to stay. The hotel's ambiance was also impressive, making our experience seem even better.

We chose a table, and the waiter took our order. As always, I ordered paalak paneer with rice, while my friend ordered some additional dishes.

When our food arrived, I was excited to take the first bite. However, the moment I tasted it, my excitement vanished. The dish was sour and unpleasant, unlike any paalak paneer I had ever eaten. It seemed like the food was stale and just reheated before serving.

We quickly decided to leave without eating. As we walked toward the exit, the receptionist noticed and asked, "You just arrived, and you're leaving so soon?"

We didn't want to explain much, so we simply replied, "We already placed our order. Thank you." and walked out. This experience taught me something important: words can attract people, but quality keeps them'. The receptionist's charming words made us enter the hotel, but the poor quality of food made us leave immediately.

- Speaking politely and engagingly can draw people towards you.
- However, your actions and the quality of your work determine whether they stay or leave.
- If your words and real efforts don't match, people will eventually walk away.

So, while it's important to speak attractively, it's even more important to deliver what you promise.

Many times, we judge things only by their outer appearance, assuming that the inside must be just as good. However, this is not always true. My experience at the hotel is a perfect example everything looked great from the outside, but the food was disappointing.

Similarly, in real life, when choosing a life partner, people often focus on external factors:

- A man might marry a woman just because she is beautiful.
- A woman might marry a man because he has a well-paying job.

But the true nature of a person is revealed only after marriage, when the outer charm fades, and reality sets in. On the other hand, someone may not be physically attractive but could have great character and values, yet they don't always receive the same attention.

The lesson? Things that look appealing often hide potential problems, while true value is often hidden behind simplicity.

Be Careful with Advertising

When people have free time, they often watch television, where they are bombarded with attractive advertisements. Companies spend millions on celebrity endorsements and marketing strategies to make their products look appealing. However, the actual quality of these products rarely matches the way they are presented.

Consumers often fall for deceptive advertising, spending money on things that turn out to be disappointing. This is why we must be cautious and aware, rather than blindly believing what we see.

The Power of Silence

A great comedian or artist knows how to entertain while delivering a meaningful message. They understand what the audience wants to hear and express their ideas accordingly. Interestingly, silence can sometimes be more powerful than words. I learned this from my own life earlier, I used to talk a lot, but people didn't seem interested in listening. When I began to spoke less in attractive way, people started paying attention. This doesn't mean we should stay silent all the time. Instead, we should listen more because true learning comes from listening, analysing, and then speaking thoughtfully.

Loose Talk

The Mistake of Speaking Without Thinking.

When we speak, we often do so without understanding the situation or the person in front of us. A foolish person speaks carelessly, anywhere, at any time, without considering the impact of their words.

Have you ever noticed someone avoiding eye contact, scratching their head, or speaking in a low, unclear voice during a conversation? This makes it difficult for the listener to understand them.

The Importance of Communication Skills

Good communication requires, Eye contact with the listener. A balanced tone not too loud, not too soft. Clear articulation so that the message is easily understood.

A Lesson from a Job Interview

A few Years ago, I applied for a call centre job. During the interview, the interviewer asked me:

"What is the role of customer care?"

He gave me 30 seconds to answer without pausing.

"Customer means people who are in distress, and care means taking care of them. So, customer care means taking care of people who are suffering."

While my answer made sense in a funny way, it was not professional. It made me realize that when we speak in a professional setting, we need to choose our words carefully.

Speaking effectively is not just about using words; it's about using them wisely. A well-spoken person engages their audience, while careless words lead to misunderstandings. Whether in personal life, job interviews, or social settings, our tone, confidence, and clarity matter just as much as our words.

Think Before You Speak

Once, while working in a textile company, I had to visit the manager for some reason. At that moment, two supervisors came to the General Manager (GM) with a conflict. Both were angry with each other, and it showed on their faces. One supervisor remained calm, while the other started complaining aggressively about his colleague. In his frustration, the second supervisor repeated the same abusive words that the first one had used against him. Now, you might be wondering. how did the manager handle the situation?

The angry supervisor was immediately fired from the company. The calm supervisor was only scolded and sent back to work. This situation teaches us an

"Important lesson"-

Control Your Words, or Face the Consequences. Many people do not think before they speak. Even when they have to complain about someone, they do it in an unprofessional and reckless manner. This can backfire and cause them more harm than good.

Later, the fired supervisor regretted his actions, realizing that he should have controlled his words instead of reacting emotionally.

In Bhagavad Gita (17.15) it is said:

अनुद्वेगकरं वाक्यं सत्यं प्रियप्रितं च यत्" Anudvega-karaṁ vākyaṁ Satyaṁ priya-hitaṁ ca yat Which means:

"One should speak in a way that does not disturb others, and one's words should be truthful, pleasing, and beneficial."

Similarly, another Sanskrit saying advises:

"सत्यं ब्रूयात प्रियं ब्रूयात, सत्यं अप्रियम् न ब्रूयात"

Satyam bruyat priyam bruyat, satyam apriyam na bruyat
Which Meaning:

Speak the truth, Speak in a pleasant manner, But if the truth is unpleasant, remain silent . This wisdom applies in every aspect of life whether at work, home, or social settings.

If we do not control our words, even if we are right, we may end up harming ourselves instead of resolving the situation.

Think Before You Speak – Words Can't Be Taken Back

Humans make mistakes, and until they gain experience and wisdom, they often say things they later regret.

We often see in news reports how parents or family members put too much pressure on their children—whether it's about studies, career, or marriage. Sometimes, harsh and hurtful words damage their self-esteem so much that they end up taking their own lives.

On the other hand, some people use these words as motivation, change their lives for the better, and achieve success.

A Life-Changing Incident

When I was young, my little sister Priyanshu was just 10 years old. One night, she refused to study, and I scolded her a lot. The next day, she was bitten by a snake, and we lost her forever.

Even today, I remember that night and think If only I had spoken to her with love... If only I hadn't scolded her so much..." Many times, we say things in anger that don't seem wrong at the time. But later, when we lose our loved ones, we deeply regret our words.

A Lesson from Buddha – Don't Respond to Insults

Once, Gautama Buddha was teaching his disciples under a tree. A man from a nearby village came and started insulting him. Buddha remained calm and ignored him. Even the village chief arrived and cursed Buddha, but he still stayed silent. When they finally exhausted themselves, Buddha smiled and asked: "If someone brings sweets as a gift, but I refuse to accept them, who keeps them?"

The villagers replied, "The one who brought them." Buddha said, "Similarly, I have not accepted your insults. So, they remain with you." Hearing this, the villagers felt ashamed and asked for forgiveness.

The Power of Words – They Can Heal or Hurt There is a famous saying:

"An arrow shot from a bow and words spoken in anger never return." A physical wound may heal over time. But hurtful words leave scars that last a lifetime. So, think before you speak. If your words are kind and loving, they will build relationships. But if they are filled with anger, they will destroy relationships. If someone insults you, don't react with anger . Stay calm because time is the best answer. Choose words that inspire, not words that hurt. "Words have the power to make or break a person."

<u>Summary</u>

1. Speak with Kindness – If your words lack love and sweetness, you won't experience the joy you expect from others.

2. Positive Conversations – While talking to a relative or anyone, ensure your thoughts are uplifting and filled with positive energy.

3. Your Own Words Affect You the Most – What others say may not hurt as much as your own words. Your words can

make you happy or sad, so always be mindful of what and how you speak. Words can heal, and words can hurt.

4. Speaking is an Art – Communication is a skill that everyone can and should practice. It is simpler than it seems.

5. Start with Appreciation – If a conversation begins with mutual appreciation, both people will naturally want to listen to each other.

6. Speech Defines a Person – A person's intelligence remains unknown until he speaks. That's why it's said, "Even a fool appears wise until he opens his mouth."

Chapter 9
The Necessity of Spirituality

"One should not remain engaged in the pursuit of material advancement alone, as it does not bring true happiness. Instead, strive to free yourself from these material bindings and embark on your spiritual journey. Only then will you find joy, for this is the sole source of true bliss and happiness."

–Bhaktivedanta Swami Prabhupada (December 20, 1974, Bombay)

Understanding Spirituality

In the past eight chapters, we have explored the essential aspects of leading a successful life. We have understood that in order to navigate life effectively, one must first become aware of its realities. For this, proper guidance, a positive mindset, and renewed energy and confidence are necessary. We have attempted to comprehend this from both an internal and external perspective.

Now, let us delve into the concept of spirituality–what it truly means and why it is essential in our lives. Everything you have learned in this book so far has been a journey leading to this final chapter. In fact, I wrote this entire book just to express the ideas contained here. You will find astonishing real-life experiences that, once understood, can simplify your life even further. After all, simplicity is the hallmark of true humanity. Many incidents in my life affirm this truth what you seek, you will find. When you embark on a journey to discover yourself, everything else starts losing its significance.

I was searching for answers to my deepest questions, along with a peaceful environment where I could pause and reflect. I didn't know what was right or wrong I was simply moving forward, like a traveller lost in the crowd, unaware of its destination.

Along the way, some people offered me food and shelter for the night, while others treated me differently. I always carried a bag full of books, sometimes selling a few to afford a meal. But where I would sleep at night was always uncertain sometimes a government office, near a school, in a garden, an open field, a railway station, or even in a remote village or town. If I travelled far, I would spend the night by a river or the sea, only to resume my journey at sunrise. I had no fixed destination, no clear idea of where I was heading I was just walking.

One morning, as I strolled along the seashore, a few lines of poetry emerged in my mind, as if whispered by the waves themselves...

Life, stop, where will you take us, Some paths have been covered, some are still left.

Let me take some rest, I am naïve, foolish,

I kept trying to learn and understand from you and kept walking with you.

It is not that my paths were deserted, I met some strangers,

but the ones I met,

I did not meet them at all.

Life, you wanted something else, I kept doing something else, now I want to know you,

Come sit, let's talk for a while, Maybe you too must be tired, You tired me out,

Just wait for a while more Life, stop, where will you take us...

When a person becomes tired of worldly things (and the suffering that comes with them), wealth, luxury cars, grand houses, and a comfortable life start to feel insignificant. These things lose his meaning because the person realizes they are temporary. Becoming too attached to them seems foolish, as they can lead to more suffering. Instead, the person begins searching for something beyond material pleasures something eternal. Such type of people long for a love that seems nowhere to be found. Their awareness remains at a lower level, and they constantly strive to elevate their consciousness. No matter where they go, they find themselves caught in a web of deep thoughts, unable to find a place where they truly belong.

They visit various institutions in search of peace, carrying countless unanswered questions. They seek answers from different people but remain unsatisfied because the responses lack the depth and sincerity they expect. This is why they keep wandering, searching for something more. Lost in uncertainty, they sleep anywhere day or night without fear of death. They have come to understand that this body is a gift from nature and will one day return to it. Their journey is a search for a place where they can find true happiness.

"What is the true purpose of this body?" they wonder.

As they wander, they read many books, hoping to find answers to the questions that trouble their inner self. Their mind remains in a constant state of unrest. They do not hesitate to take on any task and seem willing to go to any extent to find meaning.

Whenever they meet an elder whether in their family, village, or city they ask about life:

- How is your life going?
- How do you live?
- How has your journey been so far, and how do you feel now ?

They ask countless such questions. Yet, both internally and externally, the answers they receive are often disappointing whether the person is rich or poor. In fact, the wealthiest individuals often seem the most troubled.

The Endless Search for Happiness

Everyone is searching for something wonderful to make their life happy and fulfilling. But where can one find true joy and satisfaction? The desires of life never seem to end one fulfilled desire leads to another, then another, and so on. There seems to be no final destination. Over time, as people chase these desires, their physical strength diminishes, and one day, it comes to a halt. Yet, the mind keeps striving, always wanting more.

You may have heard the story of a man who wished for a pot full of gold coins from the Kalpavriksha (the wish-fulfilling tree). The tree granted him not just one but seven pots filled with gold. However, it also gave him an eighth pot that was only half full. The man took all the pots home but became obsessed with filling the eighth one completely. He worked tirelessly, day and night, only to die before he could ever fill it. In this pursuit, he forgot about the seven pots already full of gold.

The lesson is simple: humans rarely feel satisfied with what they have. Their desires are so consuming that they forget to enjoy the present moment.

During my travels, I faced several accidents, but each time, I narrowly escaped. Looking back now, I can't help but laugh it seems as if fate had its own plans for me. Walking down unknown roads at night was naturally frightening, yet whenever I lay on the ground and looked up at the sky, the moon and stars brought a gentle smile to my face. I felt grateful to be alive.

I travelled from one state to another, often without a ticket. Sometimes, kind strangers on the train would help me with money. I also noticed that Indian train ticket examiners (TTEs) were often compassionate. When they saw someone struggling, they understood their situation and let them go. However, this didn't always work in my favour.

While wandering through the road of Delhi to Noida, One evening, intense thirst struck me, and as I searched for water, the hours passed until it was 9 PM. That's when I found myself near the ISKCON temple in Noida Sector 33. It was Saturday, March 26, 2022. I had only heard of ISKCON temples before, I was sure that I would get some water here .

However, there was a problem. The security guards at the entrance refused to let me in. As I stood there, I noticed people coming out of the temple holding prasadam in their hands. A deep desire to enter the temple arose within me I couldn't turn back now. It was my first visit to an ISKCON temple, and leaving without going inside didn't feel right. I approached the security guard again and requested entry. I had a small bag with some clothes and books, which I placed before him, assuring him that I would return soon. Finally, I was allowed inside. The temple was just magnificent from the inside as it appeared from the outside. A sense of peace filled me as I stepped in. I noticed people receiving prasadam and sat among them. As I took my first bite, I realized I had never tasted anything like it before. There was something special about this prasadam as if it carried a divine essence. A thought crossed my mind: If God blesses me, I will get to eat this every day.

I looked around at the temple walls and saw paintings depicting different forms of the Lord, showcasing his divine childhood pastimes. But to me, they were more than just paintings they evoked a deep, indescribable emotion within me.

For the past three years, I had carried a copy of the Bhagavad Gita with me, searching for answers. Yet, I had not found them until now.

Finding Answers at the Feet of Krishna

The teachings of the Bhagavad Gita, spoken by Lord Krishna to Arjuna, had always intrigued me. And now, here I was, standing in Krishna's very own temple. A voice from within seemed to whisper, Could this be the place where I find the answers to my questions?

As I looked around, I noticed two devotees dressed in dhoti and kurta, speaking to each other with great humility and respect. Their words carried a sense of warmth and peace. I stood at a distance, listening intently, and after a while, I gathered the courage to approach them. Introducing myself briefly, I was met with the same kindness and gentleness in their response.

One of them informed me about an upcoming Umang Seminar at the temple the next day March 27, 2022, at 5 PM where thousands of people would gather. He invited me to attend. I agreed but was left with a strong desire to ask him more questions. However, it was late, and though I needed to leave, I had no idea where I would go.

Their words amazed me. There was so much love in their expressions, something I had never experienced in my interactions with others. They spoke different there was a rare sincerity in their demeanour. I felt a deep urge to meet them again. I asked one of the devotees about their name, and he told me, "he is Jiva Gopal Das Prabhu". In just a few moments, I felt as though I had encountered an ideal personality someone who radiated wisdom and compassion. And as time passed, it was through him that I finally found answers to my long-standing questions. A few months later, I accepted him as my Shiksha Guru (spiritual teacher). He taught me the wisdom of the Bhagavad Gita with great simplicity and clarity. Even today, I continue to study The Gita with deep reverence, striving to implement its teachings in my life.

I observed something remarkable compared to the people I had met outside, the devotees in this temple were kinder, more welcoming, and full of grace. Yet, I did not take long to adapt to this new environment.

Slowly, I began stepping into a spiritual way of life, seeking a deeper understanding of the true philosophy of existence. After seven years of wandering, I had finally found the right place to learn. But life still held many challenges, and resolving them was urgent. I wanted to stay in the ashram and dedicate myself fully to understanding the philosophy of life. For this, I chose the Bhagavad Gita as my guiding light and sought the refuge of my teacher, Jiva Gopal Das Prabhu, to help me grasp its wisdom with ease and clarity.

After spending some time in this peaceful environment, putting my feelings into words is nearly impossible but I have made a small attempt.

The Righteous Path (SadMarg)

**As a wanderer, I roamed, in search of the righteous way,
Lost in thoughts of what to do with this life each day.**

Watching the sun rise, seeing flowers bloom, Witnessing the restless mind and the body's changing tune.

What have I not seen since the journey began?

Nature's laws are unique, bound by karma's plan.

**As a wanderer, I roamed, in search of the righteous way,
Each moment, my mind swayed in life's marketplace, But how do I understand myself in this material space?**

Who am I? Why am I here?

What is the purpose of this life so dear? Seeking answers to these endless queries, I wandered on, lost in my worries.

Yes, it is true birth, death, old age, and disease are set,

Then why hesitate to renounce greed, illusion, anger, and regret?

I never stopped, nor did I bow,

As a wanderer, I roamed, seeking the righteous road.

Talking to flowers, listening to birds' sweet tunes,

Meeting strangers in cities and villages under the moon.

Hope still lingers, like an unquenched thirst,

As if the thirsty one finally finds water, life finds its true worth.

Now my soul feels pure and bright, As if everything has come into sight.

It feels as though I've truly begun to live, Like false illusions have ceased to exist. Like deceitful friends have drifted away, And a true companion has come to stay.

It feels as though... I am finally alive. With every step, He walks beside me, Holding my hand, guiding me kindly.

The stones on the path have turned into flowers, The destination now seems within my powers.

That final moment is drawing near, It feels so close, so bright, so clear.

It feels as though... I am finally alive. It feels as though... I am finally alive.

As you all know, in the past, ashrams were simple huts or cottages in the forests or far from kingdoms But with the advancement of time, everything has changed in this modern era. However, the Vedic education system and the tradition of the Guru-disciple relationship have remained the same.

What is spirituality?

The word spirituality comes from the Latin word "spiritus," which means breath, symbolizing life. It is a wonderful gift and manifests within us through our being. The simplest definition of spirituality is: Spirituality is a philosophical aspect of life that elevates human consciousness with a divine force." In other words, spirituality is the knowledge of the beyond things that transcend the material world.

Every living being on this earth must go through birth, aging, illness, and death. This is inevitable, and no one can escape it. Some wise individuals say that if suffering didn't exist, there would be no need for spirituality. Just as hospitals are necessary for treating illness, spirituality serves as a healing process for the soul.

The foundation of spirituality is peace and joy. Sadhguru Jaggi Vasudev explains spirituality as: "Something that cannot be taken away by death."

Our body and mind belong to nature because they are derived from it. However, the spiritual process transcends life and death it happens within our inner self, the 'I', which is the soul. The body is a loan taken from the earth, and after death, it will be reclaimed.

In Sanskrit, the word Adhyatma (Spirituality) is formed by two words: Adhi + Atma , meaning "to gain mastery over the soul."

Srila A.C. Bhaktivedanta Swami Prabhupada, the founder of the International Society for Krishna Consciousness (ISKCON), explains that the term Atma refers to the body, mind, and soul. Spirituality, therefore, is the harmony of the body and mind. Since the body and mind are formed from material nature, spirituality is the path to aligning them with the higher self. In the Bhagavad Gita (Chapter 8, Verse 1), when Arjuna asks Lord Krishna: O Lord, what is spirituality (Adhyatma) or the soul (Atma)?Lord Krishna answers in Verse 3:

"The eternal nature of the living being, its Sanatan (eternal) quality, is its spiritual essence."

In its purest form, spiritual consciousness or Krishna consciousness is about being in service to the Supreme Being.

Why is Spirituality Important ?

In the Bible, Jesus Christ says:

If you build your house on sand, it will collapse with the first storm. But if you build it on a solid rock, no storm can break it."

This analogy perfectly explains the importance of a strong foundation in life. Spirituality acts as that solid foundation. Without it, we are like a house built on sand vulnerable to temptations, fears, and emotional storms. But with a spiritual foundation, we remain strong and unshaken, no matter what challenges life throws at us.

Radhanath Swami, a disciple of Srila A.C. Bhaktivedanta Swami Prabhupada, says:

"The ideals we hold sacred in life can only stand strong if we have a firm inner foundation. Otherwise, we will be swayed by temptations, fears, and emotional turbulence, ultimately leading to our downfall. That foundation must be spiritual."

He further explains that a spiritual foundation brings stability and integrity, no matter what situation we find ourselves in.

As Martin Luther King Jr. once said:

If a man has nothing worth dying for, he has nothing worth living for. Spirituality gives life meaning, direction, and strength. It helps us navigate difficulties with wisdom and stay anchored in peace, no matter how strong the storm.

"Sharpening the Axe: The Importance of Spirituality"

Every living being in this world is engaged in some kind of work no one is completely inactive. You may have heard the story of the "woodcutter"

One day, a woodcutter was cutting trees in the forest. A young man happened to pass by and noticed that the woodcutter was drenched in sweat, struggling to chop down a tree. It was clear that he had been working for a long time.

The young man approached him and asked, "What are you doing?"

Frustrated and exhausted, the woodcutter replied angrily, "Can't you see? I'm cutting this tree!" Without another word, he continued his work. The young man observed him for a while and then asked, "Can I see your axe for a moment?" When he examined it, he realized that the blade was blunt. He then advised the woodcutter, "Why don't you sharpen your axe first? It will make your work much easier."

The woodcutter had never thought of this before. He took a moment to inspect his axe, then decided to go home and sharpen it. The next day, when he returned to the forest, he was amazed what once took him an entire day now took only a few hours! With his sharpened axe, he was able to cut more trees in less time and sell more wood in the market. Soon, he was able to meet all his family's needs. A few months later, the same young man happened to pass by again. Seeing the woodcutter from a distance, he noticed how happy and content he looked. As soon as the woodcutter saw him, he ran up to him, fell at his feet, and said, "Because of your advice, my life has completely changed! Today, I have everything I need for my family." Initially, the woodcutter was spending all his time and energy working hard, but he never paused to sharpen his axe. However, once he did, he was able to accomplish much more with much less effort and he finally had time to enjoy his life with his family.

Most people live their lives like that woodcutter constantly working, struggling, and pushing forward without stopping to sharpen their most important tool: their mind and consciousness. They are so busy surviving that they forget to truly live.

How Spirituality Helps

Spirituality is like sharpening the axe of our mind and awareness. It helps us develop wisdom, clarity, and purpose in life. Instead of blindly working hard, spirituality teaches us to work smartly with a sense of direction and meaning.

When we take time to sharpen our inner awareness, we can navigate life with ease, efficiency, and happiness just like the woodcutter who finally learned the power of a sharp axe.

Benefits of Being Spiritual

In this material world, spirituality offers countless benefits. Yet, some people with an atheistic mindset question the existence of God, saying, "I have never seen God, so why should I believe?"

But the principle of God is simple:

"First, have faith, and then you will see me."

Unfortunately, ignorant people fail to realize that the air they breathe, the sunlight, water, fire, and even their own breath everything is sustained by a divine force. That is why we should have unwavering faith and devotion in God. Some people argue, "If God is everywhere, why visit a temple or a spiritual place for worship?" While this statement may sound logical, we need to understand that human senses are incomplete. Our eyes can see only to a limited extent, and our ears can hear only within a certain range. Likewise, all our senses have limitations. But God is limitless and perfect. So how can imperfect senses perceive a perfect God?

To experience divine power, we must purify our senses through spiritual practice. Only then can we truly connect with God, bringing peace and happiness into our material life as well.

Scientific and Physical Benefits of Spirituality

Indian scriptures describe Navadha Bhakti (Nine Forms of Devotion) in Srimad Bhagavatam (7.5.23-24):

- Shravanam (Listening to divine stories)
- Kirtanam (Chanting God's name)
- Smaranam (Remembering God)
- Padasevanam (Serving His feet)
- Archanam (Worshipping)
- Vandanam (Offering prayers)
- Dasyam (Being His servant)
- Sakhyam (Seeing Him as a friend)
- Atma Nivedanam (Complete surrender)

Whatever we do in life should be connected to spirituality with complete faith in God.

A study at the University of Pennsylvania revealed a fascinating connection between spiritual practices and physical health. According to Indian scriptures, when a person bows down completely (Sashtang Pranam) before God in a temple 11 to 15 times daily, it helps prevent osteoporosis (a disease that weakens bones).

Similarly, the power of chanting God's name has both physical and mental benefits. People often assume that spirituality is only for attaining liberation (moksha), but in reality, it strengthens both body and mind.

Another study by Professor Andrew Newberg at the University of Pennsylvania observed people of different ages over 20 days. They meditated for 10 minutes daily, focusing on their preferred form of God while chanting His name. After the study, MRI scans and brain mapping revealed: Children's memory power increased by 15-20%Teenagers and young adults gained better memory and higher self-confidence. Elderly participants (aged 70-80) experienced physical and mental health improvements.

If just 10 minutes of daily spiritual practice can bring such significant benefits, imagine how powerful a fully spiritual life can be! Ancient Indian sages and scriptures have always emphasized spirituality, and modern science is now proving it to be 100% true.

Summary

1. A strong spiritual foundation provides stability, integrity, and a higher purpose in life.
2. Spirituality enhances physical, mental, and emotional well- being.
3. Every action in life should be infused with spirituality, or else it remains meaningless.
4. As the Bhagavad Gita (8.3) explains, the eternal nature of the soul (Jivatma) is spirituality itself.
5. A spiritually awakened person sees all beings with equal respect and compassion.

Thus, spirituality is not just about faith or devotion it is a practical tool for a happier, healthier, and more meaningful life.

Author 's Thoughts & Quotes

1. If a person learns how to live life before actually living it, life becomes joyful. Even when faced with serious problems, they can handle them with ease.
2. Only when the mind is calm can a person distinguish between right and wrong.
3. If you are facing a tough challenge, understand that something better is on the way. If you have a disagreement with someone today, strive to ensure it doesn't happen again tomorrow.
4. No being in this world is perfect. Trying to become perfect is foolish. Accept yourself as you are and fulfill your duties because only God is truly perfect.
5. When talking to someone, make sure your thoughts are elevated and filled with positive energy.
6. If a person cannot be happy with themselves, they should not expect to be happy with anyone else.
7. If you cannot respect yourself, how can you respect others? And without respecting others, how can you expect others to respect you?
8. A person's thoughts do not become noble and pure overnight; they must be refined through human values.
9. "Failure" is just another form of success. If you fail while striving for your goal, try again. If you fail again, try once more. Continuous effort makes success even more meaningful.

10. I was searching for my loved ones, but I never tried to connect with myself.

11. Most of our problems start because we think too much about others. In reality, our problems are small, but by overthinking, we make them bigger.

12. The moment you realize, "I am not an ordinary person," success will not take long to reach you.

13. This mysterious world has all kinds of people–some sweet, some bitter, some spicy. You will attract people whose thoughts align with yours.

14. If you truly want to enjoy life, never compare yourself to others. You are unique, and only those who stand out are remembered.

15. Sadness in life is like sunlight; it comes and goes. There's no need to feel hopeless or discouraged.

16. When we have no goal, every task feels tiring. But when we set a big goal and start working towards it, even laziness feels like a burden.

17. When I see people smoking or indulging in bad habits, I feel proud that I am different and better. This motivates me to work harder with determination.

18. Sometimes, life throws difficult questions at us, and we don't find answers immediately. In such moments, patience and silence are key.

19. What others say doesn't hurt us as much as our own thoughts. Our own words can make us happy or sad. So, we should be mindful of our words to avoid hurting others.

20. If your words lack love and sweetness, you will never experience the joy you expect from others.

21. While maintaining relationships, be mindful of boundaries. Don't let anyone dominate or overpower you.

22. When you find an inspiring role model, your entire perspective on life changes.

23. If someone becomes an obstacle in your path to success, let them go no matter who they are. They will never truly understand your journey.

24. When meeting a stranger, don't waste too much time talking. Just a brief introduction is enough. If they try to argue or criticize you, simply listen, appreciate them, and suggest meeting another day. They will surely come back to you.

25. Since you are already a part of life's grand play, play your role in such a way that you become an inspiration for generations to come.

26. Being serious all the time isn't good. Laugh openly whenever you feel like it it will help you feel stress-free.

27. Never postpone a task for tomorrow if it needs to be done today. Do it immediately because you exist today, not tomorrow. Who you were yesterday is not who you are today.

28. If someone in your life does not support your positive thoughts and constantly discourages you, it's better to be alone than to stay with them.

29. Make it a habit to dance daily it keeps you fit and helps reduce stress.

30. When you take a big step in life, even your family and friends might not support you. Don't feel bad; they have never thought big. Your life is yours, and the decisions should be yours too.
31. If bridges can be built using stones inscribed with God's name, then no goal in life is impossible when cantered around God.
32. The world appears as we choose to see it. However, our minds are so full of negativity that we fail to notice the positive things around us.
33. If a person always talks negatively about others, it reflects their own inner negativity.
34. Bowing down is not a sign of weakness; only those who are willing to bend can go far in life.
35. I distanced myself from those whose words felt like arrows piercing my heart. Now, I am happy.
36. Lose yourself within; everything you seek is already inside you.
37. Some people don't give us time because we are going through tough times. But time is watching both sides. The darkness will pass—nothing can stop the sunrise.
38. A person who learns to control their emotions cannot be easily made happy or sad. They remain balanced in all situations and treat everyone equally.
39. The joy of successfully completing a goal should be shared with others to inspire them to pursue their own dreams.

40. When observing something, calm your restless mind and use your intellect to truly understand it. This increases the chances of achieving your goals.

41. Every human has selfish tendencies, but only those who selflessly help others and constantly remember God can achieve the true purpose of life. Everything else is just showmanship.

42. Nature has given us invaluable gifts like air, sunlight, water, fire, and beauty. We should always express gratitude for these blessings.

43. Time is the only thing in life worth stealing make the most of it.

44. Don't be afraid of problems; face them head-on. Never let your inner flame die out until success bows before you.

45. When we start paying attention to small mistakes, they eventually bring big positive changes in our habits.

46. From a cosmic perspective, human life is nothing but a tiny dot. So why worry? Dance, sing, and enjoy the present moment.

47. Everyone has problems in life. But when they confide in someone, they are often ridiculed. This creates confusion about whom to trust. The issue is that people trust others' external behavior but fail to understand their deeper nature.

48. If someone doesn't respect your thoughts, don't waste your time on them even if they are a relative or a close friend.

49. Life's play is enjoyable, but death is always lurking around.

50. Never let your emotions weaken you, or they may become obstacles on your path to success.

51. Deep observation is the best way to truly understand something.

52. Every human has both good and bad habits. Unfortunately, bad habits tend to dominate more often.

53. Most people discourage rather than motivate us. Stay away from such individuals.

54. Before asking for forgiveness from others, first, forgive yourself.

55. Feeling uncertain or afraid when starting something new is natural. Don't panic face it courageously and move forward.

56. When we have a strong determination to achieve something, even the universe supports us.

57. Patience is essential; rushing decisions often leads to mistakes.

58. The human mind is as vast as a continent. Using it within a limited boundary is foolishness.

59. Let your thoughts be so impactful that anyone who speaks with you once feels inspired to talk to you again.

60. Recognize your abilities and set your goals accordingly. Success will surely follow.

About the Author

A writer and thinker (student life) Manish Mannjya got his primary education in Gayghat, a small village in Siwan district of Bihar. His ancestral property belongs to this very place. He completed his matriculation from Chandra Badan High School and intermediate from Ramanand Yadav Inter College,located near the village. After that, he completed his graduation from Raja Singh Mahavidyalaya (Siwan) under J.P. University,Saran. During his graduation he started realizing the reality of life. However, even after working in many states, he did not get stability, did not get the satisfaction that he expected and finally his conscience inspired him towards spirituality and he embarked on the path of devotion and spirituality. He then realized that this is the real happiness of life. He is fond of writing poems even before stepping on the threshold of youth. As a result, he wrote many poems in the context of life. This is his first attempt at writing a book in which he has tried to shed light on various problems, challenges and solutions of human life and has also shared his life experiences so far. The writing style is simple and understandable which can be read by people from adolescence to old age.

Heartfelt thanks to all the readers!